CROSS-COUNTRY SKI GEAR

MICHAEL BRADY

THE MOUNTAINEERS
SEATTLE

The Mountaineers: Organized 1906 ". . . to explore,
study, preserve and enjoy the natural beauty of the Northwest."

Published by
The Mountaineers, 719 Pike Street
Seattle, Washington 98101

Published simultaneously in Canada by
Douglas & McIntyre Ltd., 1875 Welch Street
North Vancouver, British Columbia V7P 1B7

Manufactured in the United States of America

Portions of this book have appeared in the Norwegian Ski
Council's Cross Country Handbook. Used by permission of
the Norwegian Ski Council.

Cover by Galen Rowell, from Great Circle Expedition
(Mt. McKinley), 1978. Drawings by Odd R. Pettersen and
Robin Lefberg. Designed by Marge Mueller.

Library of Congress Cataloging in Publication Data

Brady, M   Michael.
   Cross-country ski gear.

   1. Cross-country skiing—Equipment and supplies.
I. Title.
GV855.5.E67B7   688.7'6'93   79-26249
ISBN 0-916890-89-9

904405.90.7

To Ivar Halvorsen,
Ski racer, coach and craftsman,
Who taught me
that there is more to a pair of skis
than skiing on them.

CONTENTS

PREFACE

Knowledge is of two kinds. We know a subject ourselves, or we know where we can find information upon it.
—Dr. Samuel Johnson, April 18, 1775

One of the absurdities of the present age of cross-country skiing, or, for that matter, any type of skiing, is that skiers often seem either totally confused by or totally preoccupied with equipment. Neither extreme leads to enjoyment of skiing.

In days now lost in history it was simpler. Everyone who skied understood skis and ski equipment well. They either saw skis being made or made skis themselves. If a ski or a piece of equipment failed to do as they wished or broke, they changed it or fixed it, to suit their skiing needs. There was harmony between the craftsmanship behind ski equipment and the practice of its use.

Those days are gone forever. Skiers are now removed from the creation of the products they use. But people are still people and can ski, and snow is still snow and can be skied upon. So the need for appreciation, for knowledge of ski equipment still exists. This book is dedicated to that goal.

There are many approaches to providing information on the equipment for a sport or an activity. The two currently most popular are perhaps the *commercial approach* and the *market overview*.

In the commercial approach, a firm, group of firms, or public relations organization puts together consumer information, concentrating of course on the brand or brands involved. Repair manuals published by automakers are extreme examples of the commercial approach: they are really useful for only one make, and often for only a few models of automobiles.

In the market overview, a publication such as a sports magazine tries to give the reader an overview of what can be found in the shops this month, this year, or this season. The effect is somewhat like that of a catalog, sometimes in text, sometimes in tables or charts.

An offspring of the market overview is the "what to look for" approach, which aims to aid informed buying.

This book is a guide to the equipment of a specific sport—cross-country skiing—yet it uses none of these approaches. It could be called a handbook, a manual, a text, or an encyclopedia (although it is not alphabetically ordered) of the subject. It includes the background material on cross-country skis, equipment, and apparel, useful to those who wish to extend their knowledge beyond that of the average user. And because it also covers equipment for ski jumping, it spans the entire recreational and competitive spectrum of Nordic skiing. It is a guide to the subject itself, useful to ski-shop personnel and interested skiers alike.

Portions of the content of this book have been adapted from *The Norwegian Ski Council Handbook of Cross Country Skis and Ski Equipment* and its supplements, compiled and edited by the author for the NSC personnel workshops, in 1976 through 1979. Permission granted by the Norwegian Ski Council for the use of this material is gratefully acknowledged. Credit is also due Ned Gillette, who suggested subjects to be covered and approaches to be used in parts of this book. Finally, Jakob Vaage's fine sense of the historical perspective and attention to detail has added accuracy without which this book would somehow be incomplete.

M. Michael Brady

INTRODUCTION

Cross-country skis, equipment, and apparel are simple in principle and simple to use. That's the way it should be. So this is a guidebook to simplicity: basics are its approach.

There are 11 chapters, each covering a single topic. Chapter 1 is a short overview, placing cross-country in the spectrum of skiing. Chapter 2 is a guide through the array of available equipment, a summary on how to buy or to advise someone on buying in an informed manner. The next chapters are devoted to the details. Chapters 3 through 8 are on skis, boots, bindings, poles and apparel. Chapter 4 is on the systems for matching boots and bindings, the only two items of equipment that must mate and work together, as automobile tires must fit wheels. Chapter 9 is on waxes, but not on waxing, as this is a *what-is*, not a *how-to* book. Chapter 10 presents some of the ancillary paraphernalia of cross-country skiing: packs, pulks, roller skis, and emergency gear. Chapter 11 fills out the Nordic skiing spectrum with an overview of ski jumping equipment. Finally, there's a Glossary of the terminology, the lingo of Nordic skiing.

None of the materials or basic processes used in manufacture are unique to the ski industry. However, they may often seem unfamiliar, either because they are described by trade names or because their other, more common, uses are not known. Therefore, all materials, products, and processes are called by their generic names in this book, and trade names now in common use are

---

KEEP THE SPORT SIMPLE

"During the last few years, the equipment problems have become more and more urgent, especially through the work put in by the [FIS] Equipment Committee. It is evident that it is necessary today to have certain norms governing the equipment, and it seems also the manufacturers are interested in this. Only, let us not complicate modern skiing too much. The norms for cross-country skiing can and should be simple, and the Cross Country Committee is proceeding in this direction."

—Bengt-Herman Nilsson, Chairman
FIS Cross Country Committee, in
the *FIS Bulletin,* no. 75,
25 April 1979

identified accordingly. Also, other, more commonplace applications of materials and processes are stated, to reference the unfamiliar to the familiar: what's inside some skis is the same stuff that's on your kitchen floor, just without color and blown full of bubbles, and so on.

Trademarks and trade names used in this book are either identified as such or appear with the registry symbol ®. All are assumed to be registered; use here does *not* imply generic meaning, either by the author or by the publisher.

The metric system of measurement, prevalent in the ski industry, is used throughout.

THOUGHTS ON UNITS

Following current trends and legislation in North America, all measurements in this book are stated in metric units: centimeters and millimeters for length, grams and kilograms for weight, and degrees Celsius* for temperature. Ski lengths and widths and pole lengths, even of skis and poles manufactured in the United States, have long been stated in metric units, so these measurements are given without conversion to feet and inches. Otherwise, conversions to English units are given in parentheses, since common usage—the way most people think—is not yet geared to metric units. For instance, skiers usually think and speak of ski lengths in centimeters but know their own body heights only in feet and inches.

The Celsius degree scale is named after the originator of the temperature scale, Swedish astronomer Anders Celsius (1701-44); zero is the freezing point and 100 the boiling point of distilled water at sea level. Also called "centigrade" (one-hundred-degree) scale, probably first so by the English who, in the heyday of their dividing things by 20, 12, or 8, apparently failed to understand systems based on division or multiplication by ten. German physicist Gabriel Daniel Fahrenheit (1686-1736) was a few years ahead of Celsius and also introduced mercury in thermometers, which may be responsible for his scale being used at all, a sort of scientific PR of the times. The exact basis of Fahrenheit's scale is not known, but one account is that he took zero as the temperature of the freezing point of a salt-water solution in his laboratory and one hundred as the temperature of the human body; the solution went down the drain, and he had a fever on that day, hardly basis for a scale of measurement.

Early ski gear used in Lapland, from the title page of the book "The History of Lapland" by Johan Scheffer, originally published in 1674.

1 THE CROSS-COUNTRY PICTURE

"Begin at the beginning," the King said gravely, "and go on till you come to the end; then stop."
—Lewis Carroll, *Alice in Wonderland*

Cross-country skiing is the oldest form of the sport and in many parts of the skiing world, the most recently rediscovered. Cross-country skiing involves self-propulsion on snow: skiing on the flat, up hills, and down hills.

One of the most popular ways to indulge in the sport is skiing at cross-country ski areas. There were more than a thousand in the United States and Canada by the late 1970s, most with marked trails and many with prepared tracks. Winter wilderness attracts many cross-country skiers who prefer to ski in solitude, in untracked snow—the wintertime equivalent of on-foot backpacking. Cross-country ski racing draws the athletically inclined; it's the on-ski equivalent of distance running, with race distances ranging from 5 kilometers (3.1 miles) to 50 kilometers (31 miles) and more.

Cross-country ski equipment differs from other types of ski equipment for the same reason that a baseball differs from a basketball: its purpose is different. And the various forms of cross-country skiing involve various types of cross-country ski equip-

WHAT'S A POWER SLED?

Recent trends suggest that the existing classifications of cross-country ski equipment—racing, light-touring, touring, and ski mountaineering—are outmoded.

Maybe so. They were first contrived for articles in *Ski* magazine in the mid 1960s. This was before the worldwide cross-country skiing renaissance, and English at the time lacked suitable descriptive words. The categories followed those then common in the Nordic countries, where most of the world's cross-country skiing was done.

That these terms gained acceptance in common usage can be attributed to pure chance, or perhaps pure lack of better terms at some critical stage in the subsequent development of the sport and manufacture and marketing of its equipment in English-speaking countries. Concurrent terminology in other winter recreation has not been as consistent: in 1965, several manufacturers mounted nationwide advertising campaigns for over-snow

ment, whose characteristics differ according to intended skiing use. The major categories, from the sturdiest to the swiftest, are *ski mountaineering, touring, light-touring,* and *racing.*

Ski mountaineering equipment is, as its name implies, intended for skiing in remote terrain that, if traversed in summer, would classify as mountaineering. It is the sturdiest of all cross-country gear, the workhorse of the sport. Ski mountaineering skis are the broadest, boots are the highest (over the ankle), bindings are the sturdiest, poles have the largest shafts and baskets, and clothing is the warmest and most weather-repellent. *Touring* equipment, traditionally the standby of the recreational skier, is preferred by wilderness skiers and backpackers. It resembles ski mountaineering equipment, but is lighter, as suits its intended use in less extreme terrain. *Light-touring* equipment is now most popular for all-around cross-country skiing, especially in well-skied areas or wherever there are tracks. *Racing* equipment is available in two varieties: *"regular" racing* for skilled skiers skiing in tracks, and *competition,* for racing on well-prepared tracks.

Cross-country ski equipment has other prominent characteristics that classify: the array of types and varieties is perhaps greater than that of any other products on the market, rivaling the variety of household appliances or motor vehicles. Skis classify as *waxable,* having bottom surfaces that are waxed with ski waxes that grip and glide on snow in the various cross-country skiing strides and maneuvers, or *waxless,* having bottom surfaces that both grip and glide without ski wax.

---

power sleds, now known as *snowmobiles.*

No such change in the names for cross-country ski equipment categories seems imminent. However, improved ski, boot, binding, and pole constructions, packed and maintained cross-country tracks and trails, and widespread recreational cross-country skiing have all contributed to altering the characteristics and the array of cross-country ski equipment available. Categories more suited to today's situation perhaps are *racing* (always in prepared tracks), *in-track* recreational skiing, *wilderness* skiing (always out of track) and ski mountaineering. Suitability notwithstanding, the older names still dominate, and are used in this book. They may well persevere, as they are not absolute but are relative to each other: today's light-touring skis are narrower than racing skis of a decade ago, but today's racing skis are still narrower than today's light-touring skis, so the scale of ski and equipment types remains valid.

All items of equipment and apparel can classify as natural or synthetic. *Natural* products—wood skis, tonkin cane poles, leather boots, cotton or wool clothing—are the older traditionals. *Synthetic* products—fiberglass skis, metal and synthetic fiber poles, textile or synthetic leather boots, and synthetic-fiber clothing—are newer and, in many instances, offer advantages not possible with natural materials. Ski boots and bindings, which attach boots to skis, classify according to the standards by which they are designed, called *Nordic Norm, Norm 38, Racing Norm,* or *Touring Norm.*

Finally, the persons for whom the equipment is designed classify, much as is the case for clothing or equipment for other sports. Ski apparel, boots, and some skis are available in men's and women's models. Almost all ski equipment and clothing is available

SKIS MEAN MANY THINGS

Skis were once extremely simple objects. Up until a century ago, skis, such as the *Telemark Ski,* were utilitarian objects for over-snow transport, used in work, transportation, and recreation. Skis differed by the skills and flair of their makers, not by use or purpose.

Special-purpose skis, for ski jumping and cross-country ski racing, first appeared around the turn of the century, and "ordinary" skis were made in *terrain* and *mountain* models. These were the types of skis first listed in a U.S. catalog in 1902 by Alex Taylor of New York: ladies' skis $5, gentlemen's skis $8.

Alpine skis were developed about 1930, which completed the major ski equipment categories as they are known: *Nordic, Alpine,* and *Jumping.*

Alpine Ski equipment became more specialized as lifts became more common. Modern Alpine ski equipment permits skiing of types unheard of 40 years ago, but is also critically dependent on mechanical uphill transportation. The major Alpine ski categories follow the racing divisions of *slalom, giant slalom,* and *downhill,* along with the more recent additions of *free-style, mid-length,* and *compact.*

Ski jumping has developed into a highly specialized competitive-only sport: ski jumping equipment is used only by ski jumpers on ski jumping hills.

Nordic ski equipment, the subject of this book, has been continually developed and improved through the years but has not departed from its predecessors' basic function or purpose: Nordic ski equipment is still for use uphill, downhill, and on the flat for recreation, transportation, or work.

The first and most striking difference between the major types of ski equipment is size and weight. If you are an Alpine skier, cross-country skis

in children's and junior or youth sizes, in addition to adult models. The result for skiers is both fortunate and unfortunate. The great variety available means that you can find gear exactly suited to your skiing needs. The disadvantage is that choosing the best equipment is not as straightforward as it once was. Over 40 brands and more than 300 models of cross-country skis are now available in North America, and the arrays of boots, bindings, poles, waxes, and clothing are correspondingly large. Even if a well-stocked shop carries only a small fraction of what is on the market, the choices confronting prospective purchasers can be awesome.

Whether you are a beginner or an experienced cross-country skier, whether you dabble in the sport or are in it professionally, the key to understanding the cross-country array lies in digesting its basics, the subjects of the chapters that follow.

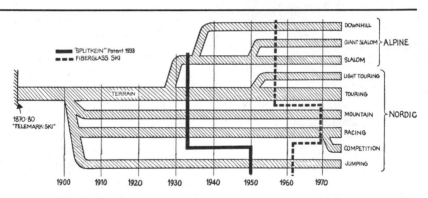

Today's skis evolved from a single type.

may seem skinny, boots old-fashioned, bindings flimsy, and poles too long. But the lightness of cross-country gear has a purpose: the less your gear weighs, the less it takes to provide your own forward power. For example, I ski both Alpine and cross-country. My Alpine gear — 190-cm fiberglass skis, step-in release bindings, size 11 plastic boots, and 54-inch aluminum poles — weighs 27 pounds 2 ounces. I ski cross-country mostly on tracks, on 210-cm fiberglass skis, toe bindings, low-cut size 11 boots, and 58-inch fiberglass poles — which together weigh 5 pounds 7 ounces. The cross-country gear I use for offtrack skiing weighs just over a pound more. If I had the necessary childhood experience or sheer guts to be a ski jumper, I would use 250-cm fiberglass jumping skis, size 11 over-ankle leather boots, and steel bindings with rubber heel wedges mounted on the skis (jumpers use no poles), with a total weight of 25 pounds 6 ounces.

2 THE WAY THROUGH THE ARRAY

Just as there are many varieties of fishing rods or bicycles, each designed for a particular purpose, there are many varieties of cross-country ski equipment, each with its purpose. Both purposes and skiers differ. So the guiding rule for choosing gear is: *The best equipment is that which best suits your needs.*
Knowing your needs is the first step to informed selection and buying, so if you don't know what they are, start selection by asking yourself four questions:
First, how and where do you ski? Are you a recreational skier or skier-to-be, who skis mostly at cross-country ski areas, on prepared

EQUIPMENT TYPES

Racing – used in tracks

Skis: Waist width: 44 mm (minimum regulation width) to 48 mm, little or no sidecut; Weight: 2 lb. 6 oz. to 2 lb. 14 oz. for a 210-cm pair.
Boots: Cut below ankle with leather or textile uppers. Soles of compact, hard plastic, 7 mm thick.
Bindings: Minimum-weight, 38-mm or 50-mm-wide aluminum alloy or plastic toe clips, attach to snout on front of boot sole.
Poles: Lightweight carbon fiber, fiberglass, or aluminum shafts, various small asymmetrical or round baskets, up to 3 in. diameter.
Clothing: One-piece, knee- or ankle-length stretch suits.

Light-touring – used mostly in tracks, on trails

Skis: Waist width: 46 mm to 52 mm; 0-4-mm sidecut; Weight: 3 lb. to 3 lb. 12 oz. for a 210-cm pair.
Boots: Cut at ankle like jogging shoes, some with groove around heel. Soles of compact, hard plastic, 7-mm thick, or foam plastic, rubber, or leather, 12-mm thick.
Bindings: 75-mm-wide aluminum alloy or plastic toepieces that attach to front of sole, or 50-mm-wide racing-type toe clips.
Poles: Tonkin, aluminum, or fiberglass shafts, diameters larger than for racing, baskets asymmetricalround, approximately 4 in. diameter.
Clothing: One- or two-piece knit or poplin suits, or wool or corduroy knickers, with sweater and/or shell parka top.

trails? Or are you a wilderness skier or ski mountaineer, who shuns marked and prepared trails? Or are you a racer?

Second, what are the prevailing snow conditions where you ski? Is the snow mostly wet, mostly cold and dry, or does it frequently vary from wet to dry during a winter? Do you ski mostly in deep powder snow, or mostly in settled snow?

Third, how often do you ski? Do you live in the snow country and ski every day, or do you travel to the snow and ski on weekends and vacations? Or are you an Alpine skier who skis cross-country only when the lift lines are unbearably long?

Fourth, how proficient are you? Are you just getting started, or have you been skiing all your life? Do you regard yourself as an average person, a skilled sportsperson, or an athlete?

When you have assessed your needs, select your equipment using the guidelines that follow.

Touring – used both in and out of tracks

Skis: Waist width: 52 mm to 61 mm; 8-11-mm sidecut; Weight: 5 lb. 5 oz. to 7 lb. for a 210-cm pair. Some with aluminum or steel edges.

Boots: Cut above ankle like hiking boots. Soles of foam plastic, rubber, or leather, 12 mm thick.

Bindings: 71-, 75-, or 79-mm-wide aluminum or plastic toepieces, some with heel straps or cables.

Poles: Same as light touring poles, but with larger, usually round baskets, diameters of 4½ to 6 in.

Clothing: Same as for light touring, often more robust for wilderness skiing.

Ski Mountaineering – used out of tracks, in wilderness

Skis: Waist width: over 61 mm; 9-12-mm sidecut; Weight: usually over 6 lb. for a 210-cm pair. Many skis have aluminum or steel edges.

Boots: Single- or double-layer, may resemble touring ski boots or mountaineering (on foot) boots. Foam plastic or rubber soles, often with lug pattern, 12 mm or more thick.

Bindings: 75 or 79 mm wide, resembling ski touring bindings, or with Alpine-ski-type release features, for use with heavy mountaineering boots.

Poles: Shafts as for ski touring poles; baskets round, over 5 in. diameter.

Clothing: As for mountaineering or backpacking in winter.

First and most important, your needs dictate what you can expect of your equipment. In selecting or buying, you will primarily be interested in three things: *performance, convenience,* and *durability.* How these properties are determined by equipment design and technology is the subject of the bulk of this book. But what the equipment *does* for you, on snow, comes first. This chapter is devoted to that purpose. The technology of the following chapters is summarized here; it's the minimum you need to know in informed buying, the background overview for reading the rest of this book.

Second, you'll find that compromises and trade-offs are part of selection. No one set of equipment is suitable for all skiing: you cannot race well and ski mountaineer successfully with the same gear. The situation is like that for motor vehicles: a four-wheel-drive truck is better than a Formula I racing car for off-the-road transport, but it would be a ridiculous choice for a Grand Prix race. If you can afford only one set of cross-country ski equipment at first, begin with gear suited to the most rugged skiing you do.

Your pocketbook *and* your needs as a skier determine how much you should spend on ski gear. Buying ski equipment is like buying

THE ANATOMY OF A SKI

Skis have parts, and the parts have names. The trend is now for ski makers, ski shops, and skiers to use the same simple, specific terms in describing skis, to describe ski anatomy in the same language.

Bottom: Ski surface normally in contact with snow when skiing.
Base: Material on ski bottom, extending length of ski.
Top: Ski surface opposite the ski bottom.
Topsheet: Material on ski top.
Sidewalls: Side surfaces, located between ski bottom and ski top.
Tip: Extreme forward point of a ski.
Tail: Extreme rear end of a ski.
Shovel: Forward turned-up section of ski, extending to tip.
Tail turn-up: Rear turned-up section of ski, back to tail.
Groove: Longitudinal indentation, or groove, in ski bottom.
Running surface: Base, or part of base contacting snow.
Body: Ski, exclusive of shovel and tail turn-up.
Forebody: Forward half of ski body.
Afterbody: Rearward half of ski body.
Core: Internal part of ski.
Binding area: Part of top intended for mounting of ski binding.

shoes: just as a high-quality, expensive pair of shoes is a poor choice if they don't fit your feet, the most expensive ski gear is not always the best for your needs. Once you know what to expect from your equipment and have focused on your price range, consider all remaining questions, such as brand, appearance, country of origin, availability, dealer services, and warranties. If you are in doubt at any stage of your selection process, try borrowing or renting equipment. *Ski and see.*

SKIS DECIDE

Skis are the most obvious items of ski equipment: without them, skiing would not be possible. Some ski equipment experts argue that, when buying, boots are more important: boots must fit your feet for you to be able to ski at all, but you can ski with less well-fitting skis. This is good advice to follow if you buy, or travel with, only one item of equipment: many expert cross-country skiers take only boots and ski clothing when traveling long distances and rent skis and poles wherever they ski. But skis dominate the scene: your choice of skis guides your choice of other items, because mixing items from different equipment categories degrades performance and can cause damage. Heavier touring boots and bindings can tear off racing skis; lightweight racing boots and bindings afford little control over heavier touring skis.

Generally, the wider a ski, the more area it puts on the snow, the less it sinks in, and the more stable it feels in skiing. But wider skis are also heavier, giving you more to carry along: narrower skis allow more freedom of movement in the cross-country strides.

WHAT IS A SKI?

"In essentials, the ski is a long narrow strip of straight-grained wood; hickory is very often used, owing to the difficulty of securing suitable ashwood, which is still with many the favorite material. The thickness is an inch or less; if the wood be sufficiently tough, the width, about four inches, and the length varying according to the height and choice of the wearer. The end which extends back of the heel is square, the toe is curved, not too sharply, and the tip is pointed. The wearer stands at the center, where straps attach it securely to his boot."

—J. C. Dier (editor)
A Book of Winter Sports
The Macmillan Company,
1912

Quality fiberglass skis are stronger than wood skis, so a narrower pair of fiberglass skis can be as strong and dependable as a wider, heavier pair of wood skis.

Though as slim and light as the racing skis of a decade ago, modern light-touring skis, skillfully used, are tough enough to withstand the punishment of extreme skiing. The 1977 Ellesmere Island and 1978 Mt. McKinley ski expeditions used light-touring skis and equipment with success, and with no failure of equipment.

In boots, height is the primary classification. Generally, the higher the cut of a boot, the more support it gives the ankle, and the warmer it can be made. See box, pages 16 and 17, for the major characteristics of the different categories of equipment.

After you have decided your general category, you still face an array of choices in selecting skis and other items of equipment. The best way to select equipment is to choose in steps, narrowing your choices with each step. (If you are a racer, turn to page 35; the rules for you are different.)

Waxable versus waxless

The first, and most important, choice you must make is whether you want *waxable* or *waxless* skis. It is not a question of whether you should wax your skis for better performance, as in Alpine skiing, but rather a question of selecting a basic type of ski. Cross-country skis must grip *and* glide on snow, not just grip, as shoe soles or automobile tires, or just glide, as Alpine skis or sled runners. Skis are made with two different bottom, or base, surfaces: *waxable* skis have bases that hold ski waxes that grip and glide, and *waxless* skis have base surfaces that grip and glide without wax.

How well a ski grips and glides depends on how well its bottom surface suits the character of the underlying snow. Snow surfaces have not just one but a virtually endless variety of properties, easily a thousand or more different characteristics. This is why waxable bases are potentially the best performers, because different ski waxes can be applied in different amounts to suit different snow conditions. A waxless ski base has only one bottom surface, one approximation to all the snow conditions possible, which is a limit to performance. This is why racers use waxable skis almost exclusively.

But waxing is sometimes difficult, as when snow is in transition between wet and dry at 0°C (32°F), or when snow conditions change from wet to dry during a tour. For these conditions, waxless bases can outperform waxable bases, which is one reason why they are popular with recreational skiers, and why several models of waxless competition skis have been successfully used in racing at 0°C.

In short: for the same overall ski quality, waxless skis will seldom outperform well-waxed waxable skis, but they will always outperform poorly waxed waxable skis.

The major advantage of waxless skis is their convenience: they are always ready for skiing, with no preparation. But modern cross-country waxes are so simple to use that waxing is no longer as complex as it once was. So if you ski infrequently on changing snows, the choice between waxable and waxless skis amounts to whether you are willing to learn waxing to achieve the performance it provides. If you prefer the convenience of *not* waxing, or if you ski widely varying snow conditions, then select waxless skis.

There are three main types of waxless skis in a variety of models: patterns, inlaid hair strips, and composite base materials. If you want to know more about the bases, read Chapter 3. But if you just want to buy waxless skis that work, find out what types are most popular where you ski. Basically, you'll want skis that grip and don't slip backwards, glide fairly well, and don't ice up on the prevailing snow conditions. You may also prefer skis that make little or no noise as they glide. One check is to see what the ski rental shops in your area have in the way of waxless skis, and try to compare skis by skiing yourself. Again, *ski and see* is one of your best guidelines in buying.

In waxable skis, there are two main choices of base: wood bases on wood skis, and plastic bases on some wood and all synthetic fiber skis.

Wood bases have their traditional advantage of being the original waxless base: at subfreezing temperatures, they can grip and glide on snow with little or no wax. But wood must be prepared with tar compounds to retain its waterproofing and hold wax, which is an inconvenience for many skiers. Unprepared, wood bases can absorb water, which can then freeze and damage the base surface, weakening the ski. Wet or iced bases hold wax poorly or not at all.

Plastic bases are waterproof and, when correctly waxed, can outperform wood bases. But they have the disadvantage that they must be waxed to grip and glide on snow: without wax, they only glide, like sled runners or alpine skis. The extent of waxing needed depends on the *porosity* of the plastic on the ski base, or how well its surface absorbs wax. Extremely porous bases absorb and hold wax well, and therefore are the best performers, but they need more waxing care and attention than less porous bases.

In short, higher-performance plastic waxable bases require more care: if you are not a racer and speed is not your main skiing goal, select skis with bases that are more convenient to care for.

Wood versus fiberglass

Skis are classified according to the materials of which they are made much in the same manner as buildings. Just as a wood frame house is still a frame house, even though it may have a brick facing, it's the material in the framework, or structure, of the ski that counts. Cross-country skis are now made with either wood or synthetic fiber structures. Fiberglass is the most common synthe-

---

DON'T KNOCK WOOD

Synthetic-fiber skis with plastic bases, when correctly waxed, outperform their wood predecessors, so there's little doubt that wood skis with wood bases are passé for racing ski constructions. But for recreational and utilitarian use, the story is different.

Wood is the original waxless ski base. This is because wood is *hydrophilic* (has an affinity for water), a property that lets wood bases grip and glide on most snow conditions with little or no wax. This "waxless" property is especially good when snow temperatures are low and conditions are stable, but it even works at temperatures around freezing, the troublesome transition range for waxing, provided the snow is new. No single material functions this well; only waxed bases perform better.

So wood bases are not only for purists, for the romantics who dislike synthetics: wood bases are useful for recreational skiers uninterested in performance, those who stroll on skis, sometimes caring little for waxing.

Wood bases have at least one utilitarian advantage that no other current base material can match: the ability to withstand extreme misuse. Some armies demand that skis for their ski troops be able to withstand extreme base abrasion, such as when ski soldiers are towed behind a vehicle on a sanded road. Wood stands up to the punishment; the plastics now currently common on ski bases either melt or pick up so much sand that they subsequently are unskiable.

Wood bases do have drawbacks. Their hydrophilic property allows them to absorb water, which can freeze to ice, expand, and ruin the base, or penetrate into the structural layers and cause the ski to lose camber or warp. Also, wet wood has poor abrasion resistance, and the edges of wet wood bases can rapidly become rounded. But the advantages are still there, some of them unmatched.

tic fiber used, although other esoteric materials, such as carbon and aramid fibers, are used in high-performance competition skis. So wood versus fiberglass is one of the major choices confronting you as a purchaser of skis.

Wood skis, the traditional choice and dominant type up to 1974, are now the endangered species of skiing; they are available in diminishing numbers each season. The demise of wood is due mainly to the advantages of modern fiberglass skis. A high-quality wood ski is still better than a low-quality fiberglass cheapie, but for skis of comparable quality, fiberglass now has the upper hand.

Fiberglass skis are stronger and more durable, and many models are guaranteed against breakage. Fiberglass skis are usually better performers in both speed and turning ability, which is why they are now used exclusively in racing. (Recreational skiing follows racing, just as jogging follows competitive running.) Fiberglass skis are also usually easier to maintain than their wood predecessors, which is a definite advantage in convenience for recreational skiers. If you prefer waxless skis, your choice is essentially limited to fiberglass, as very few wood skis with waxless bases are available.

Wood skis are objects of beauty, products of craftsmen. If you love skiing, you will enjoy handling and working on them much as some sailors relish the care of wood boats. One argument in favor of wood skis is that broken ones can be repaired with ordinary carpentry tools and glues, but damaged fiberglass skis need more specialized, expert repair. Wood skis also offer other advantages (see box, page 22).

Whatever the future of cross-country skiing, it seems certain that fiberglass and other synthetic ski structural materials will take over. That's progress, for better or worse. Choose fiberglass skis if you like what they offer. But wood skis are good choices, as they are still one of the few bargains left in winter sports gear. And they give you the chance to participate in the sport in the way it once was.

Width

A wider ski feels more stable in skiing, but don't go wider than about 52 to 55 mm at the ski waist (the midpoint, underfoot) for a first pair. Wider skis are also heavier, and added weight on your feet will slow your learning of the sport. If you are an intermediate, advanced, or expert skier, select a width to suit your skiing: narrower skis for higher performance on trails and in tracks, broader skis for bushwhacking. Your selection of ski width partly determines your selection of bindings and boots, because skis, bindings, and boots should be of the same general category to best work together for optimum performance.

Side profile

Skis are made with several different side profiles, which are most easily distinguished from above when the ski is resting on a flat, horizontal surface. Traditional and still most common is *sidecut,* the hourglass shape where the ski is wider at its tip and tail than at its waist, in the center of the ski. The difference in widths isn't great, seldom more than about 10 percent, but the sidecut profile is a feature that aids *tracking,* or how straight the ski runs when pointed in one direction, and turning, especially on downhills. Racing skis, intended for use in prepared tracks, have little or no sidecut; ski mountaineering skis, intended for use in untracked snow in mountainous terrain, have the most sidecut.

The effect of sidecut, or the lack of sidecut, depends on other ski characteristics, such as how well the ski resists the twisting that can change the shape of its sides in a turn. This means that a

---

CONVERTING BY TWOS AND FOURS

Metric specifications are common for measurements of skis and ski equipment. Here are a few tricks for converting to and from the metric system:

Length: There are 2.54 centimeters to the inch, so:
— ten centimeters is about *four* inches;
— one meter is a little less than forty inches.
Remember: A person *two* meters (6 ft. 7 in.) tall is very tall. But that's a common adult ski length.

Weight: There are 2.2 pounds in a kilogram, so:
— to convert kilograms to pounds, double the number of kilograms and add 10 percent for good measure;
— to convert pounds to kilograms, divide by two and subtract 10 percent, which is almost right.
Remember: A person 100 kg (220 lb.) is a heavyweight; one half that is a lightweight. Ten kilograms (22 lb.) is a fair load to carry on your back when skiing.

sidecut profile is no guarantee that a ski is easy to turn, but for skis of equivalent construction and quality, it's a help. If in doubt, check by skiing. Try making downhill turns on a fairly hard-packed slope where you usually ski, using skis with and without sidecut. The best skis are those that make turns easiest for you, on the snow where you usually ski.

Length

Ski length should suit your height. Stand erect on a flat floor, wearing ski boots or low-heeled shoes. The correct ski length is from the floor to the palm of an upraised arm. The average lengths according to this rule are given in the table on page 34. These are the lengths that give you the best combination of stability, maneuverability, or control in turns, and performance in the cross-country ski strides.

Beginners sometimes feel more comfortable on skis 5 cm to 10 cm shorter than indicated by the upraised-arm rule because shorter skis are usually easier to turn, more maneuverable. Wilderness skiers may choose shorter skis for ease of maneuvering when bushwhacking. Tall skiers, over 6 feet 1 inch, also may select

---

Temperature: Remembering all that dividing (or was it multiplying?) by nine (or was it five?) is confusing, to say the least. Better to remember a few temperatures, and work from there.

- To convert from Fahrenheit to Celsius degrees, first subtract 32, then divide by 2 and add 10 percent.
  Example: What's 50°F, a warm winter temperature, in Celsius degrees?
  $50 - 32 = 18°$ above freezing
  $18° \div 2 = 9°$
  $9° + 10\%$ of $9° = 9.9°$
  Round off to 10°, and you're right on.
- To convert from Celsius to Fahrenheit degrees, multiply by 2 and subtract 10 percent, then add 32.
  Example: What's $-10°C$, a common temperature specification on waxes, in Fahrenheit degrees?
  $-10° \times 2 = -20°$
  $-20° - 10\%$ of $-20\% = -18°$ F below freezing
  $-18°F + 32°F = 24°F$; right on.

Some temperatures to remember? 100°F, a little over body temperature, is a little over 37°C (body temperature). 72°F is an average room temperature; that's about 20°C. 32°F, where water freezes, is 0°C.

. Correct ski length, for average adults. Children can select skis to grow into.

slightly shorter skis: seldom do even the tallest skiers choose lengths over 220 cm, which is why longer lengths are scarce.

Don't overdo shortness; there is no cross-country equivalent of the "short" or "compact" lengths of alpine skis. Shorter skis tend to be less stable and often perform less well in the cross-country strides.

Skis for children five to sixteen years old can be chosen slightly longer than indicated by the upraised-arm rule to provide ski length to "grow up to." Children two to five years old are best fitted with shorter skis, for safety's sake.

Flex and stiffness

Flex and stiffness determine how a ski translates your weight and the forces you apply in skiing into pressure on the snow. For best performance, flex and stiffness should suit your weight, skiing ability, and the type of skiing you do. This critical step in selection is often the most neglected, which is the cause of much skier dismay. Even the most skillfully waxed waxable bases or the best of waxless bases can perform poorly, making skiing less of a joy and more of a struggle, if those bases are on skis that are too stiff for your weight and skiing ability.

More than at any other stage of the selection process, this is where you may need expert assistance. Flex and stiffness are not numbers, like clothing or shoe sizes, but characteristics that determine the way a ski behaves in motion, on your feet, where you ski.

Expert skiers and skilled shop personnel usually have a "feel" for ski flex and camber, based on long experience: they can flex a pair in their hands and squeeze a pair together, base-to-base, to match skis to skiers. Even if you are not an expert, don't be afraid to flex and squeeze skis together. *Think:* would you refrain from plucking the string of a guitar or playing a few notes on a piano before purchasing? Skis move; they are dynamic objects. Flex and stiffness give them their dynamic characteristics. Knowing something about them is like knowing that a string can give a musical instrument its sound.

Flex is short for the *flexural stiffness pattern* of a ski, the property that determines the ease or difficulty with which the ski bends along its length. A ski can be divided into three main sections from front to back: tip section, midsection or *body,* and tail section. The tip section extends from the front point, or *tip,* of the ski back about a quarter the length of the ski. The tail section extends from the rear end, or *tail,* of the ski forward about a sixth the length of the ski. The word "section" is usually dropped when speaking of the tip and tail sections of the base of a ski, so *tip* means both the pointed front end of the ski and the front section of the base, and *tail* means both the squarish rear end of the ski and the rear section of the base. In these terms, you glide mostly on the tips and tails of your skis and kick from their midsection.

A good cross-country ski should have a flexible, "soft" tip that "flows" over terrain variations. A stiff tip tends to dig in, causing skis to dive down into loose snow. A tip that is too soft will let skis wander off course when gliding. The ski should be progressively stiffer towards its waist, in the middle of its body, to carry skier weight. It should be progressively softer from the body back to the tail, so the rear part of the ski will flex evenly and not chatter off bumps. But the tail should be stiffer than the tip for good ski control in turns and on downhills.

Stiffness is short for *camber stiffness. Camber* is the upward arching curve of the middle of a ski and is what distributes your weight over the length of the ski, translating it into pressure on the snow. Strictly speaking, *camber* means the curve only, but is often used to mean camber stiffness.

Camber stiffness is the property of a ski that determines how much force is required to flatten out the camber curve. When you ski, your weight is a force that pushes downward to flatten out the camber curve. Your *kick,* the push-off from your foot that propels you forward, is also a force that flattens out the camber curve. Therefore, in selecting skis, you should find a pair with a camber stiffness that matches your weight and kicking force.

Most ski factories make skis with camber stiffnesses that increase with ski length. Each length of a particular model of ski is produced with a range of camber stiffnesses suitable for the average weights of skiers using that length of that model. For instance, adult male skiers 5 feet 9 inches to 5 feet 11 inches tall usually select skis 210 cm long, so most 210-cm skis are made in camber stiffnesses suitable for skiers weighing about 150 to 175 pounds, average for the heights involved. So if you are light or heavy for your height, you may need to select shorter or longer skis to get a pair with the correct camber stiffness.

The more a ski model is intended for faster skiing, the greater its stiffness. This is because the faster you ski, the harder you must kick to propel yourself forward. Racers often kick with a force of three times their body weight or more, but at average recreational skiing speeds, skiers seldom kick with a force of more than their body weight. Therefore, racing skis are usually made stiffer than the corresponding recreational models.

When you ski, your kick will flatten out a ski with the correct camber stiffness, putting the midsection of its base in contact with the snow. The wax of a waxable ski or the irregularities of a waxless ski then dig into the snow, giving the ski the grip that makes your kick propel you forward. A ski that is too stiff will not flatten out when you kick. Its wax or waxless irregularities cannot dig into the snow well enough for good grip; your skis may slip backwards with each kick. The effect is like that of the spinning wheels of a car stuck in snow: you waste lots of power for little motion. A ski that is too soft will flatten out even when you don't kick, maybe even when you glide on both skis. Its midsection will drag on the snow and grip slightly, slowing your glide. But if you err, it's best to be on the soft side: your skis may be slow, but at least you'll make it up hills.

Snow conditions also have some effect on the ideal camber stiffness for your weight and skiing proficiency. The harder the snow, the more it can withstand the force of a ski being flattened out. The softer the snow, the more it tends to flow under the ski, to contact the ski's midsection before it is flattened out. So the rule is: stiffer skis are best on hard tracks, such as those set by machines at many cross-country ski areas; softer skis are better for off-trail skiing in deep snow. This doesn't mean that you must have two pairs of skis with different camber stiffnesses. It just means that you should select camber stiffness to suit you, your skiing, and the prevailing snow conditions where you ski.

One note of caution: *do not* select a racing ski unless you intend to race or ski at racing speeds. In addition to being relatively stiffer, racing skis often have a camber stiffness known as "double camber," in which stiffness increases as the camber curve flattens out. This property keeps the center of the base of the ski off the snow until it is literally punched downward by a forceful kick. It's what allows racers to wax ski tips and tails for glide and midsections for grip alone, a combination that's made for maximum speed. But to benefit from this characteristic, you must kick like a horse or run like a racer. So if you are not a horse or a racer, you'll slip backwards with every kick. For you, buying racing skis is an expensive way to ski poorly.

How to choose the best camber stiffness? Someday, computers may mate skis to skiers. But, as yet, there's no substitute for the human touch, for the experience of skiing and relating the way skis feel to the way they perform. Fortunately, there's a check that even the experts sometimes make in selecting skis: the paper test. It isn't absolute but it's an excellent, easy guideline.

LIGHTEST NOT ALWAYS BEST

Many cross-country skiers err in selecting gear by going too light: racing gear is the lightest, highest-performance type available, but also the most difficult to use. To attain the performance it affords, racing gear requires racing skills. This is no new development, no consequence of the newer trends in racing equipment. Experts have long admonished cross-country skiers to shy away from racing gear unless they intend to race:

" ... Just as you'd ride a Morgan horse (at least in my area) for a pleasure jaunt over the countryside and enter a Thoroughbred in the Wood Memorial, so would you use the standard sturdier, all-purpose gear for touring and use the leaner, more specialized racing outfit if speed is the criterion."

—John Caldwell
The Cross-Country Ski Book
Stephen Greene Press, 1964

The paper test: Place a sheet of paper about 10 cm (4 in.) wide under the middle of one ski of a pair resting on a flat, horizontal, clean, hard (*not* carpeted) floor. Stand with body weight equally divided on the skis, shoe tips at the ski balance points. With proper camber stiffness for recreational skiing on most snows, the paper can be moved back and forth slightly and pulled out with moderate resistance. With your weight all on one ski, the paper should be clamped fast between ski and floor. If the paper can be moved at all with your weight all on one ski, the skis are too stiff. If the paper cannot be moved at all with your weight on both skis, the skis are too soft. If you ski mostly on hard tracks, particularly in wet snow (which compacts to a hard surface more readily than cold, dry snow), then you can select skis slightly stiffer than indicated by the test. If you ski mostly in soft, untracked snow, then you can select skis slightly softer than indicated by the test. Always follow the test by flexing the skis. Remember, no test is 100 percent certain: a pair of warped planks could theoretically test perfectly, but they sure would be terrible things to ski on.

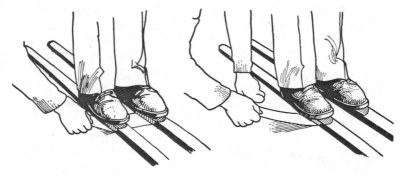

Proper camber for skier weight allows a piece of paper to be pulled out from under ski when it carries half body weight.

BOOTS AND BINDINGS WORK TOGETHER

Choosing skis simplifies the choice of boots and bindings by narrowing the selection to those that suit your skis; that are of the same general category of cross-country gear.

Boots and bindings work together like a hinge between the toe and the ski, allowing the foot to flex naturally, as if you were walking. In boots and bindings you'll be interested in *flexibility,* how easily the foot can bend forward in a boot fitted to a binding, and *stability,* how well a weighted boot, in a binding and flat on a ski, can control the ski, such as is required in downhill turns.

By far the most popular type of binding is the *pin binding,* in which the boot toe is held by an overlapping bail that presses the sole down onto protruding pins that lock into sole recesses. Pin bindings are available in a wide range of designs, some light enough for racing, others sturdy enough for major ski expeditions.

Despite the multitude of models, all pin bindings fit all corresponding boots, regardless of make or model, thanks to the *Nordic Norm,* a boot-binding standard that specifies that there are only three widths — 71 mm, 75 mm, and 79 mm — as measured at the pins of the binding or recesses of the boot sole. The 71-mm width is used almost exclusively for children's boots and bindings and 79 mm for large adult sizes (men's 13 and above) or for some ski mountaineering boots and bindings. But the bulk of adult models and sizes come in the 75-mm width.

Cable bindings, which resemble the universal ski bindings of the 1930s and which can be made more sturdy than pin bindings, are still used for wilderness skiing and ski mountaineering. But pin bindings are now made so strong that this traditional advantage of the cable binding is now minimal. Some ski troops in Europe use pin bindings, and pin bindings were used exclusively on the 85-day Ellesmere Island ski expedition in 1977, proving that the pin binding can withstand the most rugged of skiing conditions.

New to the binding-boot scene are the toe-clamp systems, originally developed for lighter weight and greater flexibility in racing. Toe-clamp bindings attach to lip extensions, or "snouts," on the front of the boot soles. Because the bindings have no side flanges alongside the boot toe, they are symmetrical (no left or right). Because the binding itself does not guide the toe of the boot, as does a Nordic Norm pin binding, boot soles are made of relatively stiff materials that resist sideways twist, for stability. Soles are thin, 7 mm (about ¼ in.) thick, for maximum flexibility.

Two types are available: the *Norm 38* and the *Racing Norm 50,* with the numbers designating the width, in millimeters, of the boot sole snout where the binding attaches. The two systems differ basically in the methods of attaching the boot sole snout to the binding.

Although excellent for and now dominant in racing, these boot-binding systems have a few disadvantages for recreational skiing use. First, the thin boot soles don't insulate as well as the thicker soles used on Nordic Norm boots, so the boots are colder on the feet.

Second, the harder sole materials, usually relatives of nylon, are slippery and skitterish to walk in. The soles of the most recent models of boots have rubber inserts to counteract slip, and insulating insoles for warmth.

Newer yet is the *Touring Norm 50,* a hybrid boot-binding system with the profile and attachment devices of the Racing Norm 50 system and the thicker (12 mm, about ½ in.) rubber or foam polyurethane soles of the Nordic Norm styles.

If you are a newcomer to cross-country skiing, stick with the Nordic Norm, at least for the time being. The system is proven, having evolved from boot and binding designs that have been around since 1928. You'll also find more boot and binding models to choose among in Nordic Norm than in the other, newer systems and can probably find suitable products for lower prices. But as you gain skiing skill, watch the other systems: you may want to switch in order to enjoy the lightweight performance that they afford.

Most makes of boots are available in lined (usually with synthetic pile) or unlined models, with leather, synthetic leather, or fabric uppers. Lined boots are warmer but take longer to dry and retain foot odor longer—certainly not drawbacks for weekend skiers. Leather is still the best all-around material for uppers, as it is for the uppers of shoes and hiking boots, because it "breathes" to allow foot moisture to escape, yet is fairly water-repellent. Rubber or plastic uppers may be more waterproof than leather, but they lack leather's ability to breathe, allowing feet to become wet in their own perspiration. Textile uppers are lighter than leather, but less waterproof. But on the other hand, they dry more quickly.

Your choice of boot depends on how you intend to ski and use your boots. If you are purely a pleasure skier who puts on boots in the morning, walks or drives to skiing, skis all day with a few breaks, and then returns home, then leather boots with rubber or foam plastic Nordic Norm soles are your best all-around bet. If you want skiing performance and lighter weight, consider boots with lightweight upper materials, such as nylon textile. Let your own foot warmth be your guide to choosing lined or unlined boots.

When buying boots, be sure that they fit snugly, yet are roomy enough for foot freedom in all skiing movements. For most skiers, this means that when wearing socks, toes should have about ⅜-inch clearance to the inner edge of the uppers. A good trick to check fit is to slip your foot into an unlaced boot and push forward until your toes touch the front of the boot upper. You should then have enough room behind the heel for the first two fingers of your

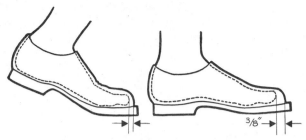

Boots should have about ⅜ inch clearance to the inner edge of the uppers to allow for forward toe motion when foot flexes.

hand. Leather boots will widen in use to fit your feet but will not increase in length, except for some leather-soled boots that stretch when wet. So if you doubt, select a pair that is a bit too narrow instead of a bit too wide.

Finally, check that the bindings can mount easily on the skis. Bindings are made with two different spacings between the rear two screws: 26 mm for bindings to be mounted on skis 44 mm to about 48 mm wide at their waists, and 32 mm for bindings to be mounted on wider skis. Don't mount bindings with 32-mm screw spacing on narrow skis, because the screws may damage the ski sidewalls. It is usually a good idea to let your shop mount bindings: they generally have the skill and the tools required. But if you are more experienced or simply want to do it yourself, see Chapter 6 for the tricks of the trade.

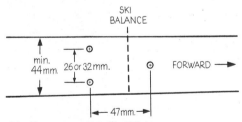

Now, most toe bindings mount with 26-mm rear screw center spacing; minimum ski width is now 44 mm.

POLES — LOOK AT BASKETS FIRST

In selecting poles, begin with the baskets. Small, angled and/or asymmetrical baskets are excellent for well-prepared, packed tracks, but sink easily into soft or untracked snow. Larger baskets are better for softer snow, but add weight. As a general rule, baskets 4 inches or less in diameter are for use on packed tracks, and baskets 4½ to 5 inches or more in diameter are better for use in untracked snow. Some pole makers offer "snowshoe baskets," large accessory baskets often 6 inches or more in diameter that clip over smaller pole baskets for more secure poling in deep snow. So if you ski both packed tracks and deep snow with the same pair of poles, pick a pair with smaller baskets and carry snowshoe baskets for off-track skiing.

Pole grips and straps should fit comfortably, not only with bare hands but with hands in all the combinations of gloves or mittens that you intend to wear.

GUIDE TO APPROXIMATE RECREATIONAL SKI AND POLE LENGTHS

	Height (feet)	Ski length (cm)	Pole length (cm)
Children	3'5"	120	Poles not
and	3'7"	130	recommended
Junior	3'10"	140	
	4'0"	150	90
	4'2"	160	95
	4'5"	170	100
	4'7"	180	105
	4'9"	185	105
	4'10"	190	110
	5'1"	195	115
	5'4"	195	120
	5'6"	200	125
Women	4'9"	185	110
	4'11"	185	115
	5'1"	190	120
	5'3"	190	125
	5'5"	195	130
	5'7"	200	135
	5'9"	205	140
	5'10"	210	140
Men	5'1"	195	120
	5'3"	200	125
	5'5"	205	130
	5'7"	210	135
	5'9"	210	140
	5'11"	210	145
	6'1"	215	150
	6'3"	220	155

Pole shafts are made of tonkin cane, fiberglass, aluminum alloy, or carbon fiber. Tonkin cane, the traditional pole shaft material, is now on the wane, and the synthetics are taking over, as they are in skis. But tonkin poles are still inexpensive and, if broken, can often be repaired at home—both advantages for the cost-conscious skier. Fiberglass shafts and aluminum alloy shafts are available in a wide range of strengths and qualities ranging from poorer than tonkin cane to far stronger and more durable; the myriad of types are discussed in Chapter 7. In short, quality usually follows price, as the shaft is the major component of a ski pole. Carbon fiber shafts are lighter than shafts of any other material, which is why they are used almost exclusively in racing. They are also stiffer, which aids precise poling—a desirable feature for any pole, racing or recreational. However, they are also more expensive than other poles, sometimes as much as five to ten times as costly as poles with shafts of other materials.

Select proper pole length using the same sort of test as used for selecting ski length. Stand on a flat floor, with an arm outstretched horizontally from your shoulder. With point, or *tip,* resting on the floor, the proper pole length is with the pole grip just under your arm, equivalent to fitting snugly under your armpit. Approximate pole lengths for various heights are given in the table on page 34.

RACERS — A DIFFERENT GAME

Racers select racing equipment for the single goal of maximum skiing speed, sometimes at the sacrifice of characteristics, such as durability and strength, that are of interest to recreational skiers.

In boots and bindings, for instance, racers select for fit, using the same general guidelines as used for selecting recreational boots and bindings. But boot insulation and waterproofing need not be as great as they should be for recreational ski boots used under the same snow and weather conditions. When they have their boots on, racers are skiing, not standing; on the move, they stay warm. And they seldom wear their boots for more than a few hours, so some waterproofing can be sacrificed for lighter weight.

Selecting racing skis and poles is a different game entirely. First, the floor-to-palm-of-upraised-hand guideline for ski length is seldom exact for racers. Ski length relative to body height, or ski length in centimeters, is less important for racers, because:

1. ski contact length, which determines the length of base that can contact the underlying snow, is more important than overall

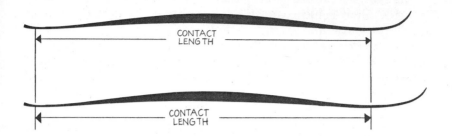

Contact length can be the same, although imprinted ski lengths differ.

length. Skis differing in overall length may have the same contact length, or vice versa.

2. as there are three different ways of measuring the overall length imprinted on a ski, skis of the same imprinted length from different factories may not be equally long. In extreme cases, different brands of ski with the same imprinted length may differ in actual length by as much as 5 cm.

3. for a racer, ski camber stiffness, which determines how forces applied by the body translate to pressure on the snow, is more important than overall ski length. Ski makers usually increase stiffness with ski length, to suit the general trend of body weight

To get stiff enough skis, a stocky racer may select long skis, and a slender racer may select short skis.

increasing with height. This is why a short, stocky racer may select "long skis" to get a pair that is stiff enough, or a tall, thin racer may select "short skis" to get a pair that is soft enough.

4. ski length influences the subjective feel of a ski on a racer's foot. Some racers prefer skis that are so long that a ski tip can never trail the opposite leg, as might otherwise happen in maximum leg extension in the diagonal stride. This is why racers with longer legs relative to their body height often select skis longer than racers with relatively shorter legs and longer torsos.

Obviously, experience is the best guide to racing ski length. If you are a racer lacking experience with different ski lengths, try the following procedure:

First, select the approximate length for your height. Use the table for recreational ski lengths or use the floor-to-palm-of-upraised-arm rule, or select skis about 30 cm (1 ft.) longer than you are tall, all of which should give you the same ski length. This is your basic, average ski length.

If you are short and stocky, add 5 cm to this average length. If you are tall and slender, subtract 5 cm from the average length.

Some racers prefer longer skis for skiing in predominantly flat tracks and shorter skis for hilly tracks. In international racing where racers are the best equipped, many have skis of different lengths to suit different course profiles. This is a moot point for

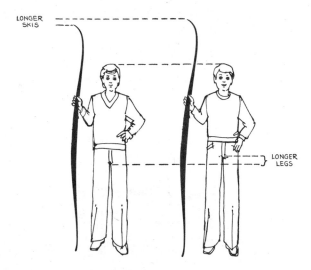

Long-legged racers may have longer strides and feel more comfortable with longer skis.

those who have to buy their own equipment but worthwhile considering if you ski mostly at one area.

Second, select ski stiffness, using the procedures explained below. If none of the skis of the length you have selected are stiff enough, go up 5 cm in length. If all are too stiff, go down 5 cm in length. If necessary, change models or brands.

Third, once you have narrowed the selection to a choice among several pairs, compare contact lengths. In general, the longer the contact length the better, for skis that otherwise suit your needs.

Stiffness: crucial

Many racing ski makers now imprint stiffnesses on racing skis, usually as numbers or letters keyed to selection charts or tables, which relate average racer body weight to dry-snow and wet-snow ski stiffnesses. Stronger racers should select stiffer skis than indicated, and less proficient racers should select softer skis than indicated.

Camber stiffness can be measured exactly on special apparatus, similar to that used by ski factories for the purpose. In function, these testing machines support the ski on a long, rigid metal bar and have a mechanism to depress the midpoint to flatten out the camber and devices to display the forces applied as electric indicators show camber curve change. At least two such camber stiffness testing machines, known commercially as *ski testers,* are now available. However, as they are fairly large and costly, they usually are used only by larger ski industry firms, such as factories, wholesalers, or major ski shops.

Lacking factory specification or exact measurement of camber stiffness, skis may be selected by trial. Start selection with the

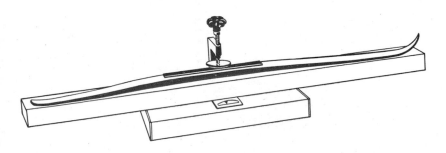

Ski tester measures camber stiffness.

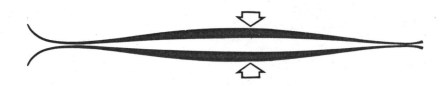

Squeeze skis together at midpoints to test camber.

paper test, as for recreational skis. But for racing, skis are stiffer than for recreational skiing. Therefore, with weight equally divided on both skis, the paper under the skis should be free to move easily back and forth for a total length of about 50 cm (20 in.) and with weight all on one ski, the paper should pull out with marked resistance. For wet-snow skis, it should pull out with little or no resistance.

The paper test relates camber stiffness to your weight only: it does not take your strength into account. So follow the paper test with a squeeze test. Hold the skis in your hands at their midpoints, base to base. If you are a normally developed cross-country ski racer, and not a weight lifter or body builder, your arm strength is proportional to your leg and overall body strength. If you can squeeze the skis together at their midpoints with two hands but not one, they have approximately the correct stiffness for your strength. Check with a one-hand squeeze: you should be able to close the bases to within about 2 mm (slightly over $\frac{1}{16}$ in.) of each other, but no more. If you can close the bases completely with one hand, the skis are too soft for your strength as a skier. If you cannot close them with a two-hand squeeze, they are too stiff.

Picking a good pair

Always check new skis for defects that may affect performance. Also, if skis you have been using seem to go bad, check for defects. The more common defects are the more easily checked: damaged base or topsheet, delamination, or damage to sidewalls. Less obvious, but most important to overall ski performance, are structural or core defects that degrade the skiability of otherwise apparently good skis.

The defects affecting performance that you can check are twist, warp, pair mate and closure, and base flatness.

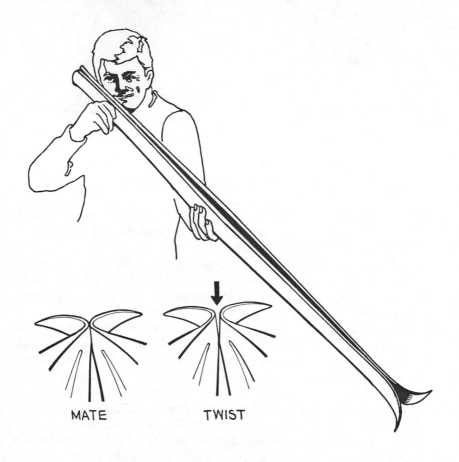

MATE   TWIST

Sight along skis to check for twist.

Check for twist and warp: Twist or warp will cause a ski to *yaw,* that is, always turn or climb out of a track instead of running straight.

Check for twist by holding a pair of skis together and sighting from tail to tip when the tails are held together. Bases should touch over their entire width at the shovel. If there is a v-shaped gap, one or both skis is twisted. Even if the skis meet as they should, both may be twisted. Check for this defect by reversing one ski, holding the pair with one tail against one tip, and resighting.

Check for warp by squeezing the midpoints of the skis together. The waists should meet exactly. If there is an offset, one or both skis are warped. Even if the waists meet exactly, both skis may be warped, in opposite directions. Again, check for this defect by

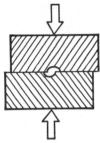

Mid-ski mismate indicates warp.

reversing one ski, holding the pair tail against tip (centering at both contact points, as tips and tails are seldom of equal width), and resqueezing the midpoints.

Check mate and closure: Sight between the bases as you squeeze a pair of skis together at their midpoints. The bases should close evenly and smoothly, with no high or low points, no gaps in between points where the bases touch. Bumpy bases wear wax unevenly and glide poorly. With the skis held completely together, check pair mate: edges should match along the entire contact length of both skis. Slight mismatch, less than half a millimeter (about 1/64 inch) on a 44-mm-wide racing ski, has little effect. But greater mismatch will cause uneven tracking, or pull to one side.

Check base flatness: For best performance, bases should be flat, although a slight curvature has little effect. Concave, or *railed,* bases wear wax unevenly and degrade ski grip; convex, or *bowed,* bases wear wax unevenly and, in extreme cases, degrade control and glide.

Check base flatness by placing a steel base scraper, or any tool with a good straightedge, on the base. Sight along the base with a

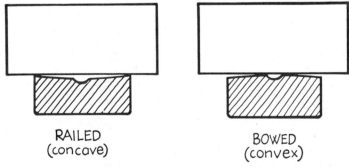

RAILED
(concave)

BOWED
(convex)

Check base flatness with a straightedge.

light behind the straightedge. If there is an opening in the center, around the tracking groove, the base is railed. If there are openings at the edges, it is bowed.

Slight curvature, less than a few tenths of a millimeter (up to about 0.01 inch) across the average racing ski base, has little effect on performance. If desired, it can be removed by scraping the bases. In average racing use, skis tend to become railed. Skis used in abrasive snow conditions, or by racers who often snowplow on long downhills, become slightly bowed with use.

Picking racing poles

Select racing poles according to performance characteristics and length.

Performance characteristics: Racing poles should be light, stiff, and durable as possible. These characteristics are available in poles with high-grade aluminum alloy, carbon fiber, or hybrid material shafts. Balance, or *swing weight,* is also extremely important in racing. Pole weight distribution should be such that the bottom part of the pole contributes as little as possible. This is because a bottom-heavy pole tends to whip like a stone on the end of a string, which makes poling imprecise and tires arm muscles. A rough check is to balance poles horizontally: other features being equal, the closer the balance point is to the grip, the better the pole is for racing.

THE "35 cm RULE" FOR RACING POLE SELECTION

Height (feet)	Average pole length (cm)
5'3"	125
5'4"	127.5
5'5"	130
5'6"	132.5
5'7"	135
5'8"	137.5
5'9"	140
5'10"	142.5
5'11"	145
6'	147.5
6'1"	150
6'2"	152.5
6'3"	155
6'4"	157.5
6'5"	160

Strap adjustment mechanisms should be easily operated with gloved hands, and straps should be adjustable to fit bare, gloved, or mittened hands. Also, for a race in cold weather, if you prefer to warm up wearing mittens and then switch to gloves for the race itself, you may want straps that can be adjusted quickly.

Length: The correct length for a racing pole is determined primarily by body height. But exact pole length must also suit a racer's body build: racers with shorter arms may select longer poles than racers of the same height with longer arms. Individual technique, how far arms extend in front of and in back of the body in the various strides, and quality and depth of tracks most often skied also influence the best pole length for a racer.

Start by following the general rule valid for recreational skiers: pole grip up under the armpit, about 35 cm (14 in.) less than body height. Lengths according to this rule, for the 2½-cm increments in length now common for racing poles, are listed in the table.

Length also depends somewhat on pole design, which determines where the hand rides on the grip and how far the pole sinks into the snow before being stopped by the basket. This is why racing pole lengths recommended by different manufacturers are seldom the same. For instance, Finnish pole makers now recommend poles 33 cm (13 in.) shorter than body height, which adds 2½ cm to the lengths listed in the table, but Norwegian pole makers stick with the 35 cm general pole length rule. Current regional or national racing styles also influence pole length selection, altering the lengths given in the table by 2½ cm or more.

The final rule is again: *ski and see.* When in doubt, try before you buy.

3 SKIS

Without skis, skiing would not be. This may be why skiers often indicate their importance by speaking of them as if they had human attributes: good, bad, fast, slow, tough, weak, skinny, fat, and a host of other adjectives used to describe people are often applied to skis. But just as a person called "tall" by a tribe of pygmies may well simply be average in North America, all such relative terms are poor descriptions because they lack precision. The best description of skis starts just as do the customary descriptions of many other things: with physical characteristics.

PHYSICAL CHARACTERISTICS

The physical characteristics of a ski determine how well it performs in its intended use in skiing. For cross-country skiing, overall performance can be broken down into *kick-glide* performance, or how well a ski performs in the strides that propel the skier forward; *tracking,* or how well a ski stays on a straight course when gliding; and *turning,* or how well a ski turns when gliding downhill or on the flat. No one physical characteristic can be singled out as being responsible for any one specified performance, as ski performance is due to the sum of all characteristics.

Ski characteristics may be divided into static characteristics—dimensions and weight commonly used to describe any object of comparable size and shape—and dynamic characteristics, which first are evident when the ski is subjected to forces, such as weighting and twisting, that occur in skiing.

Static characteristics

Length customarily is stated in centimeters and usually is the only dimension imprinted on a ski. There are three ways of measuring ski length:

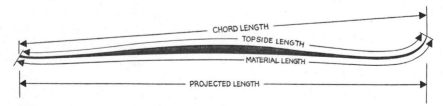

Different methods of measuring ski length.

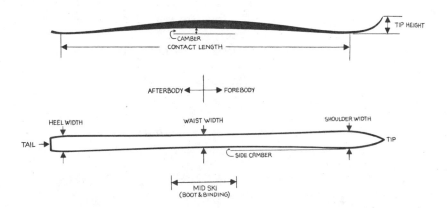

The anatomy of a ski.

Material length is the length along the base. It is the minimum length of material needed to make the ski. Topside length, measured from tip to tail along the topsheet, is essentially the same as material length.

Chord length is measured along a direct line from tip to tail.

Projected length is the horizontal tip-to-tail length of a horizontal ski.

These lengths differ, which can be confusing when purchasing skis, as few manufacturers clearly state the way they measure the length of their skis.

For instance, a ski measured and imprinted as a 210-cm ski from a factory using the prevalent material-length method typically will measure 205.5 cm chord length and 206 cm projected length. The ski is at least 4 cm shorter than a 210-cm ski from a factory using the projected-length method, and about the same length as a 205-cm ski from a factory using chord-length measurement. So *one skier's "210s" may be the same length as another skier's "205s."*

Contact length is the length of a ski base that can contact an underlying, flat snow surface. It is the length that the skier feels when skiing and is measured as the length between points where an unweighted ski touches a hard, flat, horizontal surface. For most adult-length skis, contact lengths are about 30 cm less than chord length.

Thickness, usually stated in millimeters, is the maximum thickness of a ski, measured near the waist, in the area where the binding mounts on the ski.

Width, almost always expressed in millimeters, is usually measured in three places: at the waist, approximately in the middle of the ski; at the shoulder just behind the tip where the ski first touches the snow; and at the heel, where the ski is widest just ahead of the tail. If only one width is stated, it usually is waist width.

Side profile is the profile of the ski sidewalls seen when the ski bottom is pressed against a flat surface. Skis are made with three different side profiles: *straight* (waist, shoulder, and heel approximately equal width), *sidecut* (concave sides—the hourglass shape—with waist narrower than shoulder or heel), and *boat* (convex sides, with waist broader than shoulder or heel.

In combination with other ski characteristics, side profile determines how a ski tracks and turns. Provided a ski has enough torsional stiffness to retain its side profile when weighted, sidecut will help a banked ski carve a turn in out-of-track skiing.

Camber is the upward arching curve of the middle of a ski and means either the *camber curve* itself or *camber height,* the maximum height of the curve. Camber changes when force, such as a skier's weight, is applied to a ski. The changes are described in terms of the *residual camber* and the *camber pocket,* both defined for a ski resting on a flat, horizontal surface. *Residual camber* is

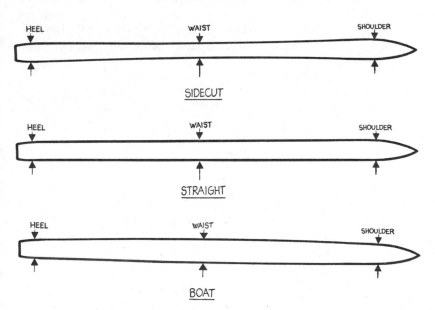

Three side profiles are possible.

Camber carries the skier.

the camber height remaining as the camber curve flattens out, and *camber pocket* is the horizontal length under the portion of the camber curve not yet flattened out by the force applied. Strictly speaking, *camber* is a geometric term only: when a ski is completely flat on the snow, it has no camber. However, in common usage, camber also implies the flexural stiffness of a ski along its camber curve.

Weight is customarily stated for a pair of skis without bindings—usually for a 210-cm adult pair or 170-cm junior pair, if length is not mentioned. Weights may be stated in grams or in pounds and ounces.

Weights of different makes of skis of similar construction and the same imprinted length can vary according to the methods of length measurement used. The only accurate way to compare weights is to compare for skis measured to have the same length by the same measurement method.

Ski weight is weight per pair without bindings.

The weights of individual pairs of wood skis or wood-core skis may differ from catalog weights because the density (weight per unit volume) of wood is not constant, but can vary depending on tree growth conditions. Ideally, ski weight should be low, to minimize the effort a skier must expend to propel skis in the various strides. However, for comparable quality and construction, lighter skis usually are weaker and less durable than their heavier counterparts, so the lightest is not always the best. Also, there seems to be a lower limit to the ski weight necessary to give skiers a feeling of stability and control. There are no kinesiological rules that dictate a minimum ski weight for proper "feel," but many top international racers now prefer to race on skis weighing 1.1 to 1.3 kg (2 lb. 7 oz. to 2 lb. 14 oz.) per pair, even though competition skis weighing 1 kg (2 lb. 3 oz.) a pair are available.

Dynamic characteristics

Flexural stiffness indicates how the various parts of a ski yield when subjected to forces, such as those encountered in skiing. Technically, flexural stiffness is expressed in terms of resistance to bending, or *bending stiffness,* which depends on the properties of and locations of the materials used in a ski and on the ski's shape and size. Bending stiffnesses are seldom expressed in numbers outside the laboratories where skis are tested; qualitative descriptions are more common. For instance, a good cross-country ski is said to have a relatively soft tip that "flows" over bumps, and to be stiffer towards its waist to carry skier weight. It should be slightly softer towards the tail to flex evenly and not chatter off bumps, but the tail should be stiffer than the tip.

Overall flex, or **camber stiffness,** describes the force required to straighten or "unbend" the camber curve. Because the straightening of a ski camber curve is similar to the straightening of a leaf spring, overall flex is technically expressed as the ski's *spring rate,* equal to the ratio of the force applied at mid ski to the decrease in camber height produced. However, overall flex is most often stated as the total load, in kilograms or pounds, required to reduce the residual camber to zero, or completely flatten out the camber curve against a flat and horizontal surface. In accurate laboratory testing, a *flattening test* with a ski not completely flat is preferable, because a specified small residual camber, such as 1 mm (0.04 in.) can be accurately measured, while the exact point

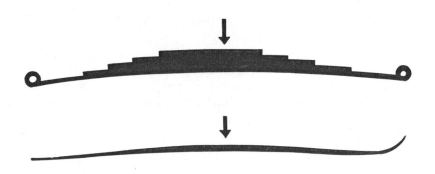

Ski camber stiffness acts like a leaf spring.

when a ski is completely flat cannot be determined accurately. Along with a ski's maximum on-snow area, determined by its contact length and width, overall flex determines how force applied by a skier results in pressure distributed on the underlying snow. Therefore, overall flex is one of the major characteristics determining kick-glide performance.

Load capacity expresses the most suitable skier weight for a desired ski performance. It is a technical term, seldom used outside ski factories.

Torsional stiffness is the resistance of a ski to twist along its axis, and usually refers to the tip portion. Torsional stiffness determines how a ski tip follows the underlying snow surface and how well a ski retains its side profile when weighted. Therefore, torsional stiffness affects kick-glide, tracking, and turning ski performances. For best kick-glide performance, tips should twist easily to follow snow surfaces. But for best tracking and greatest ease of turning, tips should be relatively stiffer so skis will retain their side profiles and not bend with the turn. Torsional stiffness is, then, always a compromise between these two opposing ski performance demands.

Breaking strength is a measure of the impact load (force of a blow) or fatigue load (repetitive force) that a ski can withstand without breaking. Impact strengths should be high enough so tips can tolerate running into bumps and mid-ski sections can tolerate weighting in dips without breaking. Fatigue strengths should be sufficient to preserve ski performances and resist camber deterioration in use.

Shear strength refers primarily to the individual material layers and joints in a ski and is a measure of the ability to withstand lateral shear loads. Delamination is the most common failure by shear in skis.

Damping describes how well a ski reduces or "deadens" vibration or "chatter" caused by motion over snow surfaces. The forces causing ski vibration increase with skiing speed. Therefore, damping is usually considered important for Alpine skis, but less important for cross-country skis, which are used mostly at lower skiing speeds. However, on steeper downhills, cross-country ski racers often move as fast as Alpine skiers, so damping is important in racing skis to counteract the vibrations that can degrade ski control.

Durability customarily implies the ability of bases, edges, and other ski surfaces to withstand wear. Aside from following trends or keeping up with newer innovations in ski design, the major reason for replacing skis is wear.

Temperature dependence indicates how the dynamic characteristics of skis change with temperature. Ideally, skis should be thermally neutral: their characteristics in the cold, on snow, should be the same as when they are warmer, such as in a ski shop. If expressed as a number, temperature dependence is usually stated as the percent overall flex, or camber stiffness changes, from +20°C (68°F) average indoor temperature to −20°C (−4°F) low skiing temperature.

The American Society for Testing and Materials (ASTM), the engineering and scientific organization responsible for production standards in the United States, is now preparing standards for technical ski specification and testing, in cooperation with the German DIN (Deutsches Institut für Normung) and international ISO (International Organization for Standardization) standards organizations. The above definitions of ski characteristics follow current ASTM proposals.

CONSTRUCTION AND MATERIALS

In principle, skis are built like I-beams or arch bridges: the major structural materials are in the top and bottom layers. These load-carrying materials, their spacing, and the methods and materials used to join them determine ski stiffnesses, strengths, and performance characteristics.

Skis are classified primarily according to the dominant load-carrying material. The materials now used are wood, various synthetic fibers, or metal alloys. Skis in which these materials dominate in the structural layers are then designated as *wood,*

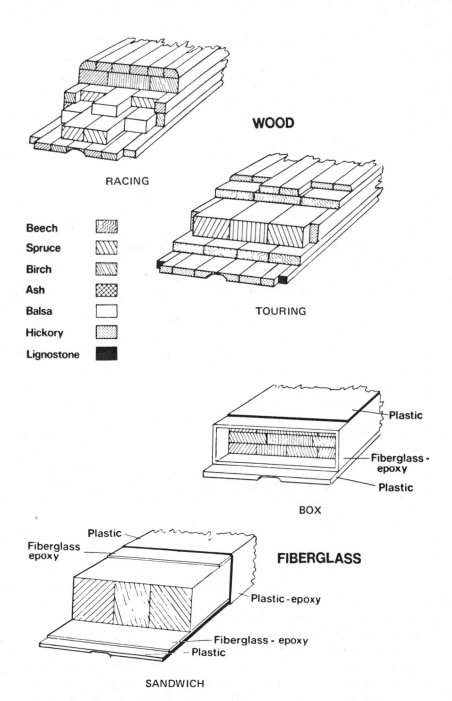

WOOD

RACING

Beech
Spruce
Birch
Ash
Balsa
Hickory
Lignostone

TOURING

Plastic
Fiberglass - epoxy
Plastic

BOX

Plastic
Fiberglass epoxy

FIBERGLASS

Plastic - epoxy

Fiberglass - epoxy
Plastic

SANDWICH

Typical ski cross-sections.

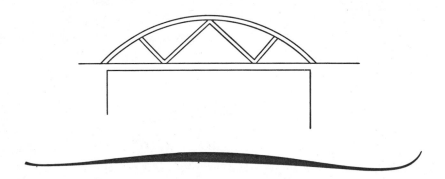

The arch is common to bridges and skis.

fiber (fiberglass, carbon fiber, aramid fiber), or *metal* skis, regardless of the type or location of other materials used. A wood ski with fiberglass reinforcement in tip, tail, and binding areas is still a *wood ski,* because wood is the load-carrying material. Designations such as "plastic skis" or "epoxy skis" are therefore meaningless unless the structural materials are specified, because most plastics and most resins, such as epoxy, cannot alone carry the stresses in a ski.

Virtually all available Nordic skis are now either wood skis or synthetic fiber skis with the trend continuing to grow toward synthetic (mostly fiberglass) skis, since the racing breakthrough at the World Championships in Falun, Sweden, in 1974. Therefore, only these two major types will be discussed further.

Wood skis — the traditionals

Wood skis are composed of many laminations, a construction technique first used around 1910 but first commercially successful in the early 1930s. Laminated skis were first developed to be stronger and more resistant to warp than solid wood skis but later also proved to be lighter.

Laminated wood skis are built up of several horizontal layers, each comprising five to eight laminations, glued together with grains reversed to counteract warp. These layers are bonded together in a press that gives the ski its shape and camber. A finished ski can contain 30 or more individual laminations.

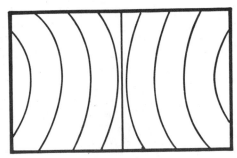

Alternating the grain of adjacent laminations opposes warp.

The top and bottom layers are the dominant load-carrying layers and therefore are made of stronger woods than the center, or core, layers, which act more as fillers and are less important for ski strength. Generally, the more laminations or greater use of stronger woods, the stronger and better-quality the ski.

Lamination is an expensive woodworking process. Only one-quarter to one-third of the wood a ski factory uses goes into finished skis. The rest is rejected in inspection or ends up as chips and sawdust from the woodworking machines.

STICK TOGETHER

The first successful laminated wood skis were made by and used by racers from Trysil in eastern Norway, near the Swedish border, around 1910. However good the laminating concept, these skis were hardly commercially feasible products. The laminations were bonded together with the glues of the day, which were not waterproof. When wet, the skis literally came unglued.

Better constructions and lamination techniques were developed in the early 1930s and patented independently by various inventors in Norway and the United States*. By coincidence, urea-formaldehyde resin adhesive, the first truly waterproof glue for wood, was developed and made commercially available also in the early 1930s. The simultaneous development of the lamination technology and the glue to stick the laminations together marked the start of modern ski making.

After production based on the patents was under way, an earlier, nearly identical patent was found; issued in Japan in 1915, it apparently had been forgotten, for the glue to make it work had not been available.

Björn Ullevoldsaeter, Ski, U.S. Patent 1,993,636, granted March 5, 1935, on application of March 1, 1934 in United States and January 18, 1933 in Norway; and Raymond C. Anderson, Laminated Ski and the Process of Making the Same, U.S. Patent 2,038,530, granted April 28, 1936, on application of May 13, 1933.

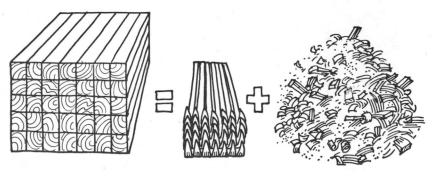

About a quarter of the wood a ski factory uses goes into skis.

The woods: Of the approximately 4,000 woods now in commercial use, only eight have been found suitable in ski making. The woods native to Europe—ash, birch, beech, poplar and spruce—are the historical standbys of the ski making art. Hickory, imported into Europe from North America and first used in skis around the turn of the century, was the supreme wood for quality skis of all types, Alpine and Nordic, in the heyday of the wood ski. Latecomers are the tropical woods, balsa and obeche.

Hickory is the strongest, most durable, but also the heaviest (specific gravity* of the dry wood is about 0.77) of the woods used in skis. It is used mostly in bases and structural layers. Hickory is now both expensive and scarce in good ski-making grades. Most of the hickory in skis imported into the United States and Canada comes from North America and thus has made two trans-Atlantic trips by the time it arrives in finished skis. As a ski base, hickory has better grip and glide without wax than any other wood.

Birch is stable, holds wax better, and is lighter (specific gravity about 0.58) but far less durable than hickory. Before epoxy-tar coated bases became common in the late 1960s, birch was the most common wood used for racing ski bases. It is also used in core, top, and side laminations.

Beech has high impact strength, is heavier (specific gravity about 0.68), and has a harder and more impervious surface than birch. Therefore it is used for top outside edge laminations and as a binding-screw anchor, as it has good screw-retention characteristics.

---

*Specific gravity is the ratio of a material's weight per unit volume to that of water. Materials with specific gravity less than 1 float; those with specific gravity greater than 1 sink.

Ash is slightly lighter than beech (specific gravity about 0.68), and is stiffer than hickory relative to its weight. It is used for top and core laminations and for bases.

Poplar is one of the lightest European woods (specific gravity about 0.41), and its tensile strength equals that of spruce. It is a stable, easily worked wood, used mostly in cores.

Spruce is a resilient, light wood (specific gravity about 0.44). It has good tensile strength but low resistance to wear, and therefore is used only in cores.

Balsa is an extremely light wood (specific gravity about 0.13). It is the weakest wood used in skis, but its light weight makes it useful in core laminations or as a filler.

Obeche is light (specific gravity about 0.35). It has a strength between those of balsa and spruce and is used in cores.

Base problems and their solution: Wood bases can wear rapidly, especially in abrasive snow conditions, such as crust and ice. Wood bases can absorb water, which then can freeze to ice, which expands and can destroy the base surface. Many material and production techniques have been used to overcome these disadvantages of natural wood bases. All involve altering, treating, or coating the base wood. There are three principal techniques:

Compressed beech: *Lignostone* (from the Latin *lignum,* meaning wood) and *Permagli* are trade names for beech wood compressed to approximately half its original volume under heat and pressure. Lignostone, the more compressed of the two (specific gravity about 1.38) is durable, with a wear resistance about seven times that of hickory, and is therefore used for edges. Since it glides well and is relatively impervious to water, it is also used for runners on sleds and pulks. Permagli is used as a base material. Because it is also relatively impervious to water, it contributes to a ski's stability and resistance to warp and loss of camber. But it lacks natural wood's ability to grip and glide on snow without wax.

Resin-impregnated birch, under trade names such as *Neswood,* is more durable and more impervious to water than natural wood. But, like Permagli, it lacks natural wood's ability to grip and glide on snow without wax.

Epoxy-tar coatings are the fastest bases available on wood skis. When waxed, they have excellent glide. With wax worn off, they still have some grip in cold, dry snow conditions, as do natural wood bases. Epoxy-tar coatings on wood bases were the most used racing ski bases in the late 1960s and early 1970s, prior to the "fiberglass breakthrough" of 1974.

Other parts: Fiberglass-reinforced plastic inserts are used in some wood skis to strengthen tips and tails and to provide binding screw anchors. Plastic is used in wood skis in edges and tip and tail protectors. Aluminum alloy is used for edges and tip and tail protectors. Steel alloys are used for edges on some mountain skis.

Synthetic-fiber skis — The new generation

Synthetic-fiber skis have structural layers of materials belonging to the large class of *composites* —man-made materials comprising fibers, fillers, and resins. Most composites use glass, aramid (for *ar*omatic poly*amid*e, chemically a distant cousin of nylon), carbon, or boron fibers embedded in epoxy or polyester resin, and various fillers to achieve the desired material properties.

Most common composites, such as SMC (Sheet Molding Compound, used for lightweight automotive body and trim parts) and FRP (Fiberglass Reinforced Plastic, used for pleasure boat hulls),

---

ABOUT PLASTICS

Plastics are organic (carbon-containing) materials that can be formed into shape by heat and pressure and retain that shape when the heat and pressure are removed. Plastics classify either as *thermoplastic,* which can be resoftened and remolded repeatedly without alteration of basic properties, and *thermosetting,* which cannot be resoftened after the initial heat-and-pressure shaping. Among the first plastics were celluloid (1892), a thermoplastic, and bakelite (1909), a thermosetting plastic.

The major ingredients of plastics are binders, plasticizers, fillers, pigments, and various additives.

Binders, which give plastics their chief characteristics and usually their names, are made up of long chainlike molecules called polymers. Binders may be natural polymers, cellulose (the binder for celluloid), or synthetic resins polymerized (built up from smaller molecules called monomers). *Plasticizers* are added to binders to increase flexibility and strength. Fillers are added to impart particular characteristics, such as impact strength or hardness. *Pigments* add color. *Additives* give special properties and often are the only differing component among trade-named plastics of the same type. Plastics may also be treated, such as with radioactive irradiation, to produce special characteristics.

The ingredients and manner of their combination determine the type and properties of a plastic. Plastics of the same type and general properties may have different properties, depending on the size of their binder polymer molecules. The sizes of polymer molecules, which are among the largest known, are expressed in terms of their molecular weights. The

use either randomly oriented chopped fibers or fiber mats. Their properties result from the particular combination of fiber, filler, and resin involved.

Ski structural layer composites differ from most other composites in that material strength and stiffness are primarily due to the embedded fibers, of which at least one set is longitudinal, continuous along the entire length of the ski. The fibers are bonded in place in a resin *matrix*, which gives the structural layers their form. This is why finished synthetic-fiber skis are classified according to the fibers in their structural layers, not by the matrix materials. Designations such as "epoxy skis" have been used, based on the argument that the ski contains about three times as much epoxy resin by volume as it does fiber. But such designations are misleading because they fail to mention the materials responsible for ski properties.

Structures: There are two main types of synthetic-fiber ski construction: *sandwich* and *box.*

---

molecular weight of a molecule is the sum of the atomic weights of its constituent atoms, expressed in *amu* (*a*tomic *m*ass *u*nits); it can be calculated from the molecular formula.

Perhaps the most familiar molecular formula is that of water, H_2O. The approximate atomic weight of hydrogen is 1 amu and that of oxygen is 16 amu, so the molecular weight of water is $2 \times 1 + 16 = 18$.

Polymer molecules have far more than three atoms of elements heavier than hydrogen or oxygen. Therefore, their molecular weights vary from a few hundred thousand amu to one or two million amu. These high molecular weights do not mean that the plastics are heavy; they just mean that they are made up of big molecules. The densities of most plastics used in skis are from 0.92 to 1.05 grams per cubic centimeter, which is close to the density of water, 1 gram per cubic centimeter.

Most plastics used in skis, particularly ski base plastics, are available in a range of molecular weights and physical properties. A plastic is called "high molecular" or "high density" if its molecular weight is in the upper end of the range, and "low molecular" or "low density" if its molecular weight is in the lower end of the range. A high-molecular, or high-density, version of a plastic is usually harder and more durable but more expensive and more difficult to use in production than the low-molecular version.

Most plastics are hydrophobic; that is, they repel water. However, a few special plastics, such as those used in contact lenses, are hydrophilic, or water-attracting. Plastics used in ski making are hydrophobic: absorbed water damages skis and degrades the wax-holding ability of bases.

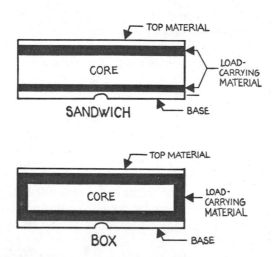

Two basic fiberglass ski constructions: sandwich and box.

The sandwich structure resembles that of a wood ski: premade veneers are laminated together, with the strongest structural materials in the top and bottom layers.

Box construction, also called by a variety of names such as torsion cell, torsion box, or monobloc, comprises load-carrying material completely surrounding a central core. Box structures are produced in many ways. Most common now is the *wet-wrap* method, in which the synthetic-fiber cloth is pressed on or wrapped around a core and then cast with epoxy resin in a mold. Another method uses *preimpregnated* synthetic-fiber cloth, which is formed and laid around a core and then hardened by heat and pressure. Still another production is *spinning*, in which ski cores are fed continuously into a machine that first draws fibers along the top and bottom surfaces and then wraps fibers around the entire core.

The basic sandwich and box construction are sometimes combined in hybrid constructions to benefit from specific materials or production techniques. One major variation of the basic sandwich construction is the injected ski. Injected ski making involves placing ski top and bottom sheets in a mold, which is then filled with a foam plastic that expands and cures to form a core. Ski cores alone may also be injection molded and then used in either sandwich or box constructions.

All the structural methods have inherent advantages and disadvantages. Sandwich-structure advantages include ability to control materials to fine tolerances, predictable curing, and precise control of ski stiffness and flex. One disadvantage is that sandwich structures may be prone to delamination if abused, which requires ski makers to control bond quality carefully.

Box-structure skis are superior in this respect: they are relatively free of delamination problems. But the trade-off for the box structure is less precise control of the resin and of the curing process. The stiffness and flex of a box-structure ski usually can only be predicted; ski pairs are matched up at the end of the production line, not before molding. Sandwich skis may be matched up in the same manner or may be made in pairs. Injection skis are usually made in pairs, in double molds that assure closer ski similarity than possible by any other production method. But present injection methods and materials pose sometimes conflicting problems in lightweight ski making. Core materials that can be injected to fill the entire space between the structural layers, out to the tapered tip and tail, and cure well for good bond tend to be heavier than noninjected cores. Lighter injectable core materials require more complex production techniques.

So no one structure type automatically assures superior skis. Ski performance and quality depend more on production quality, economics, and material quality than on basic structure.

Cores: All synthetic-fiber skis are built up on or around a core, which comprises as much as 85 percent of the ski's total volume and therefore determines its overall size and shape.

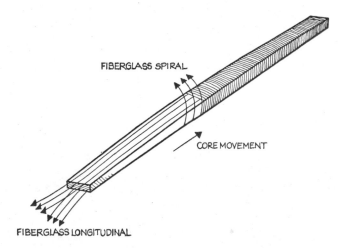

FIBERGLASS SPIRAL

CORE MOVEMENT

FIBERGLASS LONGITUDINAL

Spinning process for continuous production of box cores.

There are almost as many core constructions as there are makes of skis. This is because core design is a compromise between the desired properties of strength, light weight, resistance to warp, ease of working, quality of bond to the outer ski layers, and reasonable price. Wood, foam plastic, aluminum honeycomb, and various hybrid composites of these basic materials are used in cores.

The advantage of *wood* as a core material is that it is available in a wide range of densities and mechanical properties, has relatively high shear strength (is difficult to break across the grain), bonds well, and can be easily worked using the well-developed, traditional methods of ski making. The disadvantages are that both densities and mechanical properties vary and that some of the choice woods used in ski making are becoming scarce and expensive.

There are two basic types of wood core construction: laminated, as in wood ski construction, and mortise joining. Hybrids of these two constructions are also used, such as laminated cores built up of mortise-joined layers.

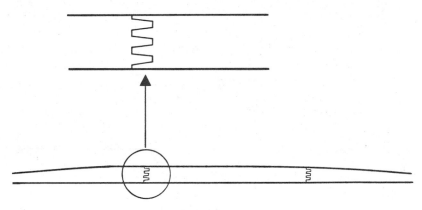

Mortise joining is used in some wood cores.

Laminated cores use mostly the same woods as used in the center laminations of wood skis: birch, beech, ash, spruce, poplar, obeche, and balsa. Aside from resistance to warp, the major advantage of laminated cores is that individual woods may be placed where their properties will be of greatest advantage in the core. Mortised cores usually use one or two woods, such as birch, ash, spruce, or poplar. Materials with little swell and relatively lower mechanical strength are used to minimize warp.

The location of different woods in composite cores corresponds to that in wood skis: beech, for instance, is often used as a binding screw anchor.

Like wood, *foam plastics* are available in a broad range of densities and mechanical properties, and many types are easily shaped and bonded. The plastics used in the foams either are foam in their normal state or are foamed by chemical or mechanical processes that literally fill the material with bubbles that form the foam cells. All foams used in cores have the prefix *poly* to their names, indicating that they are polymers. They are usually relatively rigid and may be thermosetting or thermoplastic.

The physical characteristics of a foam depend on its type and the average size of the foam cells. The larger the cells, the lower the foam density and the weaker the foam. The major advantage of foams for ski cores is their consistent and uniform light weight. The major drawback is that the foam cells have low shear strength and poor screw retention. This is why many ski makers add extra plastic, fiber, or metal sheets where the binding mounts on foam-core skis.

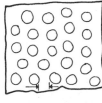
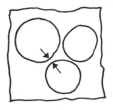

HIGHER DENSITY   LOWER DENSITY

The higher the density, the smaller the foam cells and the stronger the foam.

Four types of foam are now used.

1. Polymethacrylimide (PMI) is an acrylic plastic, a member of the polyacrylic group of thermoplastics. Among the better known acrylics are Plexiglas and Lucite. PMI, often designated in skis by the group name *acrylic*, is a lightweight, white, stiff foam in its natural state. Its stiffness suits it to stiffening cambers, thus contributing to the performance characteristics of a ski. Since PMI is relatively expensive compared to other foams, some ski makers laminate it with wood to benefit from its characteristics while holding costs down.

2. Polyurethane (PU) is a foam in its normal state, gray or black in color. PU may be thermosetting or thermoplastic and can be

61

made into both rigid and flexible objects. The major uses of thermoplastic PU are in padding for furniture and automobile seats and in mattresses. Rigid, thermosetting PU is used for insulation and furniture parts. Rigid PU is easier to work and less expensive than PMI but is also weaker on an equal-weight basis. Therefore, most PU cores use a heavier foam, with smaller foam cells. PU is currently the most common foam used for injected skis and injected cores.

3. Polyvinyl Chloride (PVC) is a thermoplastic, a polymer of vinyl chloride, and is most used as an insulator and in floor coverings. PVC foam, often called by various trade names such as Divinycell and Klegecell, is gray-white in color, light in weight, and capable of withstanding moderate pressure. It is used mostly as a filler in channels in wood cores.

4. Polystyrene (PS) is one of the older, more commonplace thermoplastics, having long been available as either a clear plastic or a stiff, white foam. The foam, best known as an insulator in refrigerators and air conditioners, is inexpensive and easily worked. However, PS foam is far weaker than the other types of foam, and therefore is used mostly as a filler in core channels in less expensive skis.

Many of the lighter foams, such as PMI, are relatively brittle and bond poorly to ski structural layers. Poorer bonds can break in shear, causing delamination. Therefore, some factories sandwich a thin wood or plastic veneer between the brittle foam core and the surrounding structural layers to provide a "softer" and more durable bond transition that absorbs the shear stresses. This layer is the second box in the "double-box" type of ski construction.

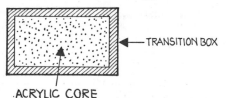

Transition layer absorbs stress between core and structural layer.

Some lightweight skis have composite foam cores, in which longitudinal strands of fiberglass roving or metal wire reinforce the light foam core, much as steel is used to reinforce concrete.

Aluminum honeycomb is light and has high shear strength and high torsional stiffness. As the name implies, aluminum honeycomb is a form of aluminum alloy expanded into many small,

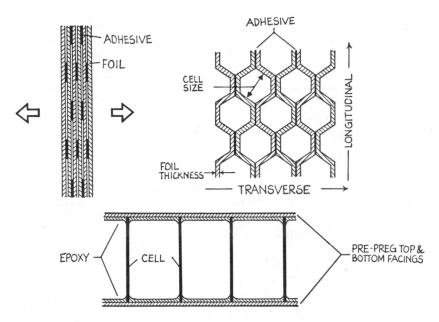

Honeycomb is expanded from aluminum alloy foil.

hexagonal cells, resembling a honeycomb. Developed for aerospace applications over 25 years ago, aluminum honeycomb, when bonded in a sandwich structure between two sheets, is one of the strongest materials available for its weight.

Aluminum honeycomb cores are produced in four steps. First, sheets of aluminum alloy foil, 0.0015 inch thick, are bonded together with parallel strips of adhesive. Then the sheets are pulled away from each other and, like the expanding bellows of an accordion, the hexagonal cells form. This is the basic, expanded honeycomb of cells, ⅛ inch across. Next, the "raw" honeycomb is profiled, or cut to final ski core shape, to form a blank that is two to six ski-widths wide and of length corresponding to the length of the finished ski involved. Finally, pre-preg fiberglass sheets, about 0.01 inch thick, are bonded with epoxy resin to the honeycomb in a press at temperatures of about 300°F, optimum for bonding to aluminum.

Honeycomb cores for other purposes, such as the structural elements of jet aircraft, use a range of foil thicknesses, 0.007 to 0.004 inch, and cell sizes, ¹/₁₆ to ¾ inch, and are usually bonded between aluminum alloy sheets. But otherwise the structures of these aircraft parts and honeycomb ski cores are similar.

The primary advantage of aluminum honeycomb cores is that they are stronger yet as light as competing core materials. However, since skis with honeycomb cores—materials developed for aerospace applications—are expensive, thus far only the most expensive recreational skis and racing skis use the technology. Theoretically, synthetic-fiber skis are more easily mass produced and therefore should involve fewer hand operations than wood skis. Since worker wages are one of the major costs in ski production, as labor costs rise this advantage should make synthetic-fiber skis cheaper. But, in actual practice, most synthetic-fiber skis, regardless of their construction, still require many hand operations in manufacture. It seems that skis, like violins, are basically labor-intensive products.

A method with considerable labor-saving potential is *injection molding,* in which cores are formed in a single operation. The resultant elimination of several hand operations has attracted considerable interest in the ski industry. Present efforts aim at developing injected cores technically equivalent to the types of cores now in more common use.

There are presently two ways of making injected core skis: molding the core alone and subsequently adding structural and outer layers, and molding the core with the structural and outer layers in one operation. Both methods use polyurethane foam plastic.

Polyurethane is a foam in its normal state. It is produced by bringing its two constituent components together and allowing them to react at a controlled rate. Carbon dioxide evolved during the process becomes trapped and forms pores, creating the foam. The larger the pores, the lower the density of the foam and the weaker its mechanical properties. The process is exothermic (gives off heat). This, combined with the heat often used in molding, produces a nonuniform density in a core: the edges are usually of higher density and therefore stronger than the interior of the core. For skis this is fortunate, as it can give cores armored sides.

Core molding is a standard method used in producing objects of plastic. Polyurethane components are injected into a mold under pressure, allowed to react, expand and fill the mold, and then to harden and cool. The advantages of the process are its inherent simplicity. Because the components can be injected from any or several places and all mold surfaces can be very smooth, the foam density can be carefully controlled throughout the core. In addition, core tips and tails or other core parts or surfaces can be precisely formed by subsequent machining operations.

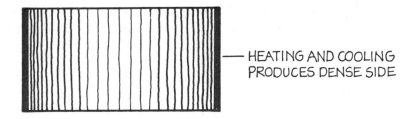

— HEATING AND COOLING
PRODUCES DENSE SIDE

Sides of injected cores can be strong.

The finished cores are then used to make sandwich- or box-construction skis, with the structural layers being bonded to the core with epoxy or other adhesives. Bonding of the structural layers in ski presses requires heat, up to 100°C (212°F), and pressure, up to about eight atmospheres. The cores must be able to tolerate these ski press stresses without deformation and therefore tend to be of stronger, denser foam. When they come out of the ski press, sandwich-construction skis must have their sides sanded to remove adhesive squeezed out by pressure. This finishing operation can remove the denser foam "armor" on the core sides, exposing the weaker core interior. Therefore, a side layer of epoxy coating or a thin plastic sheet is usually added to protect the core.

Ski molding is more complex than core molding. The most common process involves placing the top sheet, top structural layer, bottom structural layer and, sometimes, base in a mold, upsidedown. The mold is closed over the bottom of the ski, and the polyurethane components are injected from one side at the middle of the ski.

The advantages of the process are that very few operations are required subsequent to molding. The major disadvantage is that the molding itself is a difficult process to control. All the components of the finished ski must be carefully positioned in the mold. Injection can be only from the middle of a ski side, so injection speed must be accurately controlled to prevent air blocks as the foam expands towards the tip and tail of the ski. Even with the most carefully regulated injection, cores cannot be homogeneous, as foam density will vary with the spacing between the structural layers and the distance from the injection point. One reason for this is that the foam does not slide against the smooth mold surfaces, as in core molding, but must move against and finally bond to the relatively large areas of the top and bottom ski structural layers. Also, the injected foam must have a certain minimum thickness, depending on the type of foam, to resist crumbling. This is why some injected skis tend to be thicker, and therefore less flexible in tip and tail, than comparable skis of other constructions.

Structural layers: The synthetic-fiber materials used in ski structural layers are actually made up of individual fibers called *tows*. Each *tow* consists of several thousand individual synthetic fiber filaments, each about five to ten microns in diameter (a micron is one millionth of a meter, about 0.00004 inch). The synthetic-fiber tows may be *thrown* (twisted) or *spun* (drawn, twisted, and wound) and then woven into cloth, pressed into matting, or otherwise combined to form tape or strands.

Synthetic-fiber cloth resembles woven textiles but with the constituent fibers arranged in directions that suit use. "Uni-directional" fiber cloth, as often used in skis, has 90 percent of its fibers in the longitudinal direction and only 10 percent transverse. Different types of fiber may be combined, so that the cloth has the properties of one fiber in one direction and the properties of another in the transverse direction. The fibers in matting have no regular pattern but are arranged in all directions.

Cloth or matting may be (1) applied directly on cores and then impregnated with resin and cured, as in wet-wrap constructions, (2) pre-impregnated with resin for use in pre-preg constructions, or (3) fixed in a resin matrix in sheet form to be cut to laminations for sandwich constructions.

The synthetic fibers now most used in ski structural layers are of *fiberglass, carbon,* or *aramid.* By far the most common of the three is fiberglass: fiberglass-reinforced plastic has been used since the 1930s for products such as light boat hulls and shipping containers, but fiberglass was not successfully used in ski construction until the 1960s. Carbon and aramid fibers were developed for aerospace applications in the late 1960s and first used in skis in the mid-1970s. *Boron* fibers have been used in lightweight sports equipment, such as tennis rackets, but, thus far, they have not been used in production skis.

There are many different types of fiberglass, classed primarily according to the constituent oxides of the raw glass used to make the fiberglass filaments. The two classes now prevalent for fiberglass-resin composites are *E-Glass* and *S-Glass.*

E-Glass, the *E* for electrical, was originally developed as an electrical insulation material and subsequently found uses as fiberglass. It is the type most often used in skis and other sports equipment.

S-Glass, the *S* for strength, is a stronger, lighter variety developed for aerospace applications. Thus far, the relatively high price of S-Glass has prohibited its use in skis, but ski makers are now experimenting with the material, as it allows a further reduction in ski weight.

Carbon fiber, sometimes called *graphite* fiber, after the mineral, and marketed under trademarks such as Grafil®, was developed in the mid 1960s in England as a material for aircraft structures. The original breakthrough produced carbon fibers from fibers of polyacrylonitrile (PAN), a chemical polymer used in the manufacture of Orlon and other synthetic textiles. Carbon fibers are produced in tows, which are combined and used in ski production in ways similar to the corresponding processes for fiberglass.

Carbon fiber is three times as stiff as fiberglass and has 60 percent greater tensile strength. Despite its having been developed for aircraft structures, its most widespread use to date is in lightweight, high-strength sports equipment such as tennis rackets, fishing rods, hockey sticks, racing bicycle frames, ski poles, skis, and golf clubs. Golf club shafts currently represent the largest single use of carbon fibers in the world.

However, products of carbon fiber are extremely expensive and difficult to manufacture because (1) carbon fiber technology is new: the first successful products were manufactured in 1967-68, as compared to the use of fiberglass-reinforced plastics since the mid 1930s, and (2) carbon fiber is an expensive material. Research and development should improve product manufacturing and fiber production technologies. These developments, along with increased fiber production volume, are expected to lower carbon fiber prices.

Aramid fibers, marketed under trademarks such as DuPont's Kevlar®, are produced in filaments about 12 microns in diameter. Tows of aramid fibers are woven or otherwise combined, encased in resin, and used in ski structural layers in manners similar to those for fiberglass and carbon fibers.

Compared to fiberglass, aramid fibers are about 40 percent lighter and have two to three times the tensile strength, but have lower elastic limits. (The elastic limit is the greatest stress that can be applied to an elastic material without causing permanent deformation.) This means that when used in ski structural layers, aramid fibers are stronger for their weight than fiberglass but closer to aluminum alloy in behavior. For instance, tips on aramid-fiber skis can, if bent to extremes, retain a permanent deformation, as would an aluminum tip. However, aramid fibers are more easily worked and less easily damaged than carbon fiber, which makes them promising for the structural layers of light-weight skis.

Also, compared to carbon fiber, aramid-fiber structural layers have a slight hysteresis, or time lag, in reacting to forces applied. This property involves internal damping, in principle similar to the effect of shock absorbers on automobile springs. The result in performance is that when a ski is unweighted, such as at the end of the kick in the diagonal stride, an aramid-fiber ski will stay on the snow for a brief instant, longer than a carbon-fiber ski, which springs upwards almost immediately. Many racers feel that this slight lag gives better control over ski grip.

Like carbon fibers, aramid fibers are still relatively expensive, reflecting their recent development for aerospace applications. Therefore, they are thus far used only in more expensive, light-weight racing skis.

In summary, as yet no synthetic material has been found that can compete with fiberglass in its price range or in its ease of workability in production processes. So, of the synthetic fibers, fiberglass is still the dominant structural material.

Bases: Various thermoplastics are used for bases on synthet-ic-fiber skis. The design goals for a good base are good mechanical properties (such as durability and resistance to low temperature), good wax adhesion, impermeability to water, good glide, low weight, low price, and ease of cleaning, repair, and maintenance. As for wood bases, not all of these desirable properties can be achieved with a single material. Therefore, several thermoplastics are now used for bases.

Polyethylene (PE) is derived from ethylene gas. It is one of the more widely used plastics, with common applications such as in packaging, bottles, and shower curtains. It is probably the most-used ski base material, available in a wide range of types, com-pounds, and trade names, such as P-Tex and Fastex, used on both Nordic and Alpine skis. It is available in a wide range of molecular weights. The border between low- and high-molecular polyethyl-enes is customarily taken as approximately 300,000 to 350,000 amu. The most commonly used ski base polyethylenes are those in the lower end of the high-molecular range, with molecular weights of up to about 500,000. Up to this molecular weight, the polyethylene strips used to make the bases can be formed by continuous extrusion, the least expensive and most common method of forming long plastic sheets, which simply involves squeezing the material out through a die. These polyethylenes are used on many recreational waxable and waxless skis.

Less common are the polyethylenes in the upper end of the high-molecular, or high-density range, with molecular weights of 500,000 amu or more. Base strips of these polyethylenes cannot be formed by extrusion, as can those of lower molecular weight, but are machined from sintered blocks, a process far more expensive than continuous extrusion. Therefore these polyethylenes, although superior in performance, are generally used only on more expensive light touring and racing skis.

Polypropylene (PP) is derived from propane gas. It has a high melting point, 121°C (250°F), and is therefore used for objects that must be sterilized. It is light in weight and therefore used for ropes and other nautical devices that must float. As a ski base, PP resembles PE but is not as fast, especially on cold, "dry" snow. But this is not necessarily a disadvantage except for competition racing skis. Polypropylenes are available in a range of molecular weights and are durable as ski bases. Polypropylene has a surface that is dryer than polyethylene and slightly easier to wax.

ABS (a trade name for Acrylonitrile Butadiene Styrene, a petrochemical derivative of butane and styrene, the raw material for polystyrene) is available in a range of molecular weights. ABS bases glide well on almost all snow conditions but are not as fast as polyethylene bases. ABS bases hold wax well and are easy to wax when cold. They are hard and durable and resist abrasion well but usually have low heat resistance, making it difficult and possibly dangerous to use a flame for waxing or wax removal. ABS can be compounded with other materials or otherwise altered to produce

MOLECULAR WEIGHTS OF COMMON BASE POLYETHYLENES

Trade name and type	Molecular weight amu
P-Tex	
2000P	2,000,000
2000W	9,900,000
1600	620,000
Special N	210,000
Fastex	
GT100	700,000
Racing 103/2	620,000
Nordic RC 116	600,000
Nordic RC 117	200,000

base materials with properties superior to those of basic ABS; one such base material is trade-named Supernabutene, an ABS with increased butadiene content.

Most porous' bases such as polyethylene for waxable skis are roughened to aid wax adhesion. There are now two general methods used: straight sanding of recreational ski bases, and rougher grinding of racing ski bases. The ground bases require more effort to prepare and wax properly but can outperform the sanded bases, which generally are easier to wax. This is why ground bases are usually used on racing skis and some light touring skis, for best performance, and why sanded bases are usually used on recreational touring skis, for convenience in waxing.

Top sheets serve both to protect skis and to display their designs, or "cosmetics." *ABS,* in its various compoundings and base material trade names, is the most common material for top sheets, chiefly because of its low cost and good mechanical properties. However, some ski makers use transparent *polyethylene* top sheets, with all cosmetics applied to their inner surfaces before bonding on skis. This process is similar to that used to display firm names and logos on polyethylene bases. The polyethylenes used for top sheets have slick top surfaces that stay snow-free in use. *Phenolic* resins and other thermoplastics, such as Formica®, have been used for top sheets.

Sides of skis are protected in several ways. Sandwich skis with wood cores have relatively strong sides that usually need only a few coats of lacquer for protection. However, sandwich skis with foam cores need more protection and usually have ABS, polyurethane, or polyethylene sides. One variation of the basic sandwich construction essentially wraps the base material up along the sides of the ski. Box-construction skis have strong synthetic-fiber sides, which need be protected only with lacquer, although some ski makers add polyurethane or ABS sidewalls for extra protection.

Other parts: Synthetic-fiber skis may incorporate minor amounts of various plastics, rubbers, and metals, usually to achieve special features or properties. Aluminum is used for edges on some heavier touring and mountain skis, as a screw anchor on some foam-core skis, and as a tip or tail protector. Polyurethane plastic of high density is often used as a screw anchor. Phenolic resins, often impregnated into paper or wood veneers, are used as screw anchors.

Epoxy resin is used chiefly as an adhesive for bonding layers of sandwich-construction skis together; for attaching top sheets, bases, and side sheets; and as the plastic matrix for binding fibers in laminations and boxes. Combined with other materials, such as coal tar, epoxy has been used as a base coating. Epoxy-coal tar bases (introduced in the late 1960s on wood racing skis) were, in fact, the first commercially successful synthetic bases for cross-country skis. Epoxy-coal tar bases hold wax well and are less slippery than plastic bases when the wax has worn off. However, they are not as durable as plastic bases and bond poorly to the ski base layers.

The epoxy resins used in making skis harden to solid plastics, either during the manufacture of component ski parts or in the production of skis themselves, such as in the wet-wrap box ski-production processes. Therefore a finished ski usually contains more epoxy, often two to three times as much by volume as the basic structural fibers. This is why designations such as "epoxy skis" have sometimes erroneously been used.

BASES — WAXABLE VERSUS WAXLESS

Cross-country ski bases must both grip and glide on snow, as opposed to Alpine ski bases or jumping ski bases, which glide only. Therefore, cross-country ski bases are classed either as *waxable,* made to take waxes that grip and glide, or *waxless,* made with a surface that grips and glides.

Waxable bases are potentially the best performers, because wax can be changed and modified to match ski bases to various snow conditions. This is why in racing waxable skis are used almost exclusively. But waxing sometimes can be difficult, especially when snow is in the transition between wet and dry at 0°C (32°F), or when snow conditions change during a ski tour. For these conditions, waxless bases can outperform waxable bases, which is one reason why they are popular with recreational skiers and why several models of waxless skis have been successfully used in racing at 0°C.

The major advantage of waxless bases is their convenience: they are always ready to go. This is important for skiing on impulse, such as Alpine skiers who quickly decide to go cross-country upon finding that lift lines are unbearably long. But modern, wide-range cross-country waxes are so simple to use and plastic ski bases so maintenance-free that waxing is no longer as complex as it once was. Therefore, for skiers who only infrequently find themselves in transition conditions or changing snows, the choice between waxable and waxless skis amounts to whether they are willing to learn waxing to achieve the performance it provides.

Waxable bases

There are two main types of waxable ski bases: wood bases on wood skis and plastic bases on some wood and all synthetic-fiber skis. Wood bases have their traditional advantage of being the original waxless base: at subfreezing temperatures, they can have moderate grip and glide, even with little or no wax.

Birch and hickory are the woods most commonly used in wood bases. Birch is the lighter and has better wax-holding properties; hickory is the stronger and more durable but also the heavier and more expensive.

All wood bases have the disadvantage that they must be prepared, usually with compounds containing natural or synthetic tar, for water repellency and wax adhesion. Unprepared, wood bases absorb water, which not only slows glide but can freeze and damage base surfaces, weakening the ski. Wet or iced bases hold wax poorly or not at all.

In the 1960s, several wood ski bases were developed to overcome these disadvantages. *Epoxy-coal tar* coatings on wood bases offer improved water repellency and good glide and were the first commercially successful synthetic cross-country ski bases. But the thin coatings are easily damaged and not as durable as wood itself. Compressed, resin-impregnated veneers—such as those trade-named *Permagli* and *Neswood*—are water repellent, require no base preparation, and hold wax well. Their drawbacks are that they are relatively expensive and heavy.

Plastic bases are waterproof and, when correctly waxed, can outperform wood bases. But they have the disadvantage that they must be waxed to grip and glide: without wax, they glide only, like Alpine skis or jumping skis. The base plastics used are those discussed in the previous section: polyethylenes, polypropylenes, or ABS plastics.

Waxless bases

There are three main types of waxless ski base, according to the nature of the surface irregularity that provides grip on the snow: *hair, pattern,* and *composite material.*

Modern hair bases are descendants of the hair-based "kicker" skis of a century ago and are related to the climbing skins that Alpine ski mountaineers sometimes use to ascend steeper slopes.

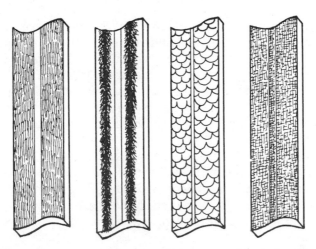

Typical ski bases, left to right: polyethylene waxable, hair-strip waxless, pattern waxless, and composite material waxless.

Hair is laid in the plastic base in strips or small rectangles, with the nap angled backwards for grip. Natural or synthetic mohair and synthetic trade-named hairs, such as Fibre-tran®, are used. Hair-strip bases work well in icy or rough corn snow conditions and have the advantage that they can be replaced when worn. But, like any garment of hair, they can absorb water and freeze. And, when frozen, they cease to function properly. Some synthetic mohairs can be made hydrophobic to repel water, and silicone waterproofing sprays are available to waterproof hydrophilic (water-attracting) hair bases.

Pattern bases have irregularities with various profiles that glide forward but grip in the backwards direction. The irregularities may be spaced individually along the base, may be closely grouped like the teeth of a file, or may be *imbricated,* or overlapping in sequence like roof tiles or shingles. The step, Fishscale®, Crown Cut®, T-Step®, and other patterns molded, stamped, or otherwise machined into the plastic bases are either *positive,* where the pattern is embossed (or raised above the base), or *negative* (where the pattern is below the base surface).

In general, performance depends more on the base quality and overall ski structure than on the method of manufacture of the waxless base irregularities. Pattern bases grip well in transition snows, as they seldom freeze. All pattern bases wear, and excessive wear degrades grip as skis age. One method of reducing wear is to make the pattern section of a tougher material, usually a plastic compound, than the rest of the base. But this method requires that the waxless section be either bonded to or inserted in the center of the base, steps that complicate production and increase cost.

Patterns rely on compressing the underlying surface for grip, which means that they may perform less well on icy surfaces, or in extremely light, dry powder snow, because their irregularities cannot compress the snow for grip. Some patterns emit a squealing sound as they glide.

Composite material bases function on a principle analogous to that of studded tires: small, backward-slanting particles grip, and the plastic in which they are imbedded glides. The major advantage of composite bases, such as the Mica® base, is that the waxless action is a property of the base material and thus is retained as the base wears.

ALL'S WELL THAT ENDS WELL

Not all developments fulfill their original intent, and the histories of all technologies contain tales of successful applications of concepts developed for other purposes. The Fishscale® base waxless cross-country ski is one such case.

In the early 1960s Skisearch, a U.S. firm, developed a "3-D Scale Base" for Alpine skis.* In principle, the scales were intended to cut drag on the snow by acting like many small hydroplanes. The goal was to eliminate the need for a groove in the base and to improve glide while increasing stability in turns. The first skis with these bases were test skied in Portillo, Chile, in 1966.

In 1967-68, Alpine ski maker Attenhofer of Switzerland experimented with the base and subsequently signed a contract with Skisearch. From 1968 through 1972, Attenhofer produced approximately 10,000 pairs of its reliable A15 metal Alpine skis with the 3D base, naming the model "Swing Jet." Two thousand pairs of Swing Jets were still in stock when Attenhofer was sold to Italian interests in 1972. Production of the model was discontinued.

Trak Inc. acquired the worldwide rights to the base from Skisearch and started using it on their *NOWAX*® line of cross-country skis in 1970. At this writing, Trak is the world's leader in waxless ski sales. Although the original 3D scale base has gone through several generations of refinements and changes, it is still recognizable as a relative of the Alpine ski base that never really caught on. The idea was there, but it was not executed correctly, nor was it used on the right type of ski.

---

*W.N. Bennett, Three-Dimensional Surface For Skis And The Like, *U.S. Patent 3,408,086, granted October 29, 1968, on application of October 25, 1966.*

The disadvantages of composite bases are that some types of imbedded particles, such as mica, are hydrophilic (moisture attracting), which can cause base icing. The problem can be avoided by treating the base with silicone base spray. Also, base glide depends on how well the tip and tail areas of the base are ground and polished smooth at the factory. However, slight tip and tail roughness can be smoothed out by applying a layer of paraffin glider wax.

All waxless ski bases have some resistance to forward glide. In high-performance models, manufacturers now compensate for waxless base drag by limiting the waxless section to the center of the arch of the ski's camber, which usually is in full contact with the underlying snow only when the ski is fully weighted, as during the kick that provides forward power in the diagonal stride. Tips and tails of these skis have smooth bases that, like waxable ski base tips and tails, may be coated with paraffin waxes for glide. This combination—gripping waxless center section and gliding, paraffin-waxed tip and tail—is the one used on the most successful waxless racing skis to date. For recreational skiers, several wax makers offer special waxless-ski glide waxes or sprays for the purpose.

SKI TYPES

Adult and junior cross-country skis classify as racing, light-touring, touring, or mountain skis. The classification of a ski into a category depends primarily on ski waist width and pair weight, as well as on physical characteristics such as ski stiffness, side profile, and torsional stiffness.

Racing skis are designed for racing and therefore are the narrowest and lightest of all cross-country skis. Therefore, for skis of similar quality and construction, racing skis are not as strong as the recreational ski types. Since the International Ski Federation (FIS) stipulates a minimum width for racing skis of 44 mm, most racing skis now have waist widths of 44 to 45 mm. Pair weights (210 cm pair) are from 1.0 to 1.6 kg (2 lb. 3 oz. to 3 lb. 8 oz.). Racing skis have stiffer cambers than recreational skis intended for skiers of the same weight, as suits their use by fast-skiing athletes, who have more forceful kicks. Ski tips are supple to move easily over all roughness in a track. Racing skis are divided into *"regular" racing skis* and *competition skis* for racing only.

"Regular" racing skis are now available in either wood or synthetic fiber—usually fiberglass—constructions. They are intended for use by expert skiers and racers, for training and racing, in fair to good tracks. They may have straight sides or a 1- to 4-mm sidecut. Wood racing skis usually have epoxy-tar-coated wood bases or thermoplastic bases bonded onto the ski. From 1970 to 1974, wood bases with epoxy-tar coatings were the most used racing bases worldwide.

Competition skis are now made only in fiberglass, carbon fiber, or aramid fiber constructions. These skis are designed for use *only* in well-prepared tracks. Ski makers strive for minimum weight, so to meet the 44-mm minimum width specified by the FIS they give the skis a straight or very nearly straight side profile: sidecut, if any, is seldom more than 2 mm. Some competition skis have a boat-shaped side profile. Most quality competition skis are now available in a range of cambers, calibrated to match racer weight. Many makers offer both dry-snow and wet-snow models, sometimes with different camber stiffness distribution and sometimes with different base materials. These properties are more fully described in the "high-performance" section of this chapter, starting on page 78.

Light-touring skis are now the most popular type, suitable for skiing trails at cross-country areas, but sturdy enough for skiing out of tracks in fairly firm snow conditions. They have waist widths from 46 mm to 51 mm, and pair weights (210 cm) are from 1.6 to 3.0 kg (3 lb. 8 oz. to 4 lb. 6 oz.). They may have straight sides or a 2- to 8-mm sidecut profile. Top sheets, bases, and structural layers are usually thicker than those of racing skis of similar construction, which contributes to ski strength. Skis in both wood and synthetic fiber constructions are available.

Touring skis are designed for travel across untracked terrain: they are light enough for general trail skiing, yet broad enough and strong enough for wilderness skiing. They have waist widths from 50 mm to 57 mm, and pair weights (210 cm) are from 2 kg to about 2.4 kg (4 lb. 6 oz. to 5 lb. 5 oz.), or more if the skis are fitted with metal edges. They usually have a 5- to 10-mm sidecut profile. Touring skis now are made in both wood and fiberglass constructions, using the same structural principles as used for racing and light-touring skis. The combination of a supple tip and stiffer tail is retained, but the greater ski width and weight makes touring skis torsionally stiffer, which aids turning but lowers their kick-glide performance compared to the other types.

Mountain skis are sturdy touring skis, designed for travel in mountainous terrain. Waist widths are 58 mm or more, and pair weights (210 cm) are 2 kg (4 lb. 6 oz.) or more. Mountain skis usually have a pronounced, 5- to 12-mm sidecut profile. Ski mountaineering has long been a no-man's land between Alpine skiing and cross-country skiing. Traditionally, Alpine skiers modified their heavier gear—for example with attachable climbing skins and special hinged bindings to permit forward boot movement—to ascend. Ski mountaineers electing the cross-country approach selected the heaviest of skis and bindings and used mountaineering boots. Now both Alpine and cross-country ski makers apparently are moving to bridge the gap between the two versions of skiing, to offer products specifically designed for ski mountaineering. Several cross-country ski makers now offer Alpine-like mountain skis, with full-length bonded steel edges and Alpine-like tip flex, and several Alpine ski makers now offer ski mountaineering models with features more resembling those of a cross-country ski, including a cross-country waxless ski base or waxable base that holds cross-country waxes. This new generation of skis averages 5½ to 6 pounds a pair (210 cm for the cross-country ski, 180 cm for the Alpine ski) and may be the harbinger of a third type of skiing, differing from cross-country or Alpine skiing as they are now known.

Junior skis and children's skis. These categories are sometimes mixed. Strictly speaking, junior skis are scaled-down versions of adult models, intended for eight- to fourteen-year-olds; children's skis are designed for tots through first-graders, more for on-snow play than for "serious" skiing. Junior skis are sometimes slightly thinner but otherwise resemble adult skis. Children's skis usually are relatively broad in relation to their length and are designed for simple strap or toepiece bindings. They are intended to be relatively inexpensive and thus, in wood models, have fewer

CHILDREN'S

ADULT

JUNIOR

Junior skis are scaled-down versions of adult skis; children's skis are broader relative to their length.

laminations than do junior or adult skis, and in fiberglass models, have simpler constructions. Some budget-priced children's skis are made of one-piece molded plastic.

HIGH-PERFORMANCE SKIS: THE WHY OF SPEED

High-performance cross-country racing skis are faster than ever. The more apparent reasons are that the newer polyethylene bases are faster than their predecessors and that advanced, more scientific waxing techniques and products are being used. This may be why these subjects dominate many discussions of ski speed.

However, the primary reason for the higher speed capability of the newer skis lies not in their bases or in waxing, but rather in basic ski design. New design knowledge and new materials have produced ski camber stiffnesses that more closely meet the performance needs of racing. These are the fine points of ski design, relevant primarily to high-performance skis, but of interest for all skis.

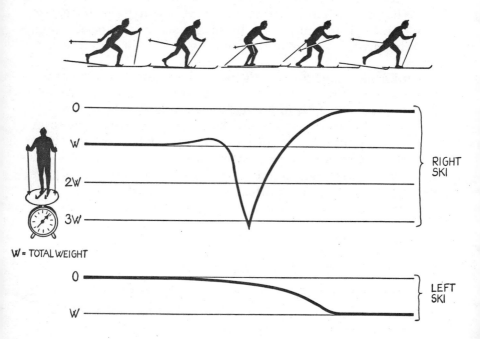

Downward force varies during stride, and is maximum – as much as three times total skier weight or more – during kick.

Pressure is decisive

Basically, all on-snow ski performance is related to how a pair of skis translates the forces of a skier's weight and motion into pressure on the snow.

Pressure is force per unit area, and weight is a force. Example: If a skier, who together with clothing and equipment weighs 176 pounds, stands still on a pair of flat, stiff planks that otherwise meet the FIS specific requirements for cross-country racing skis (175 cm contact length, 44 mm width), the total "ski" area is 154 square centimeters (23.5 square inches), and the resultant pressure is evenly distributed on the snow at 154 grams per square centimeter (7.5 pounds per square inch), roughly equal to half the pressure of the atmosphere at sea level.

Skis, unlike the stiff planks of the example, do not put even pressure on the snow. Were this not so, planks could be used as skis. The basic action of a ski is more like that of a leaf-type automobile spring: force on the center of the ski causes it to flatten out. As it flattens out, the ski puts pressure on the snow in patterns suited to the various skiing maneuvers.

In the diagonal stride, for instance, the force a racer puts on a ski is

equal to body weight when the racer glides on one ski, with the other ski and both poles off the snow;

slightly less than body weight for an instant, as the knee bends prior to the kick;

three times or more body weight for a brief instant during the kick;

zero when the ski is off the snow and the racer glides on the other ski.

A racer's ski is not simply "weighted" during a kick; it is "punched" into the snow, for the same reason that you leave a deeper footprint in wet sand when running than when walking: motion involves dynamic force.

Skilled touring skiers who ski as well as racers, but not as fast, put correspondingly less force on their skis during the kick phase, about 1.5 times body weight. Average recreational skiers may put even less force on their skis during the kick.

This is the basic reason why the cambers of racing skis and touring skis differ for persons of the same weight. For the *same kick force,* a touring ski *must* put more pressure on the snow at its

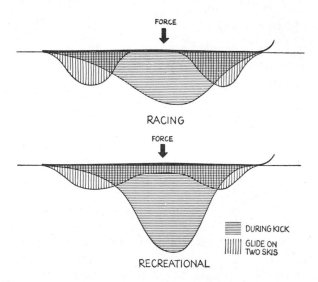

Touring and racing ski pressure distributions differ. The same force produces more pressure under the center of a recreational ski than under the stiffer racing ski.

WAXLESS RACING

Cross-country ski racing began before wax was invented, so the first cross-country ski races were, in today's terminology, run on waxless skis. Untreated wood provided the grip for these earliest cross-country racing skis. They worked fairly well in cold weather but gripped poorly on warmer, wetter snows. (This is perhaps why the first successful cross-country racing wax was a klister, for wet conditions.) Modern waxless ski bases were originally developed as a convenience for recreational skiers, and not thought of as offering the performance required in racing. But there have been exceptions.

U.S. racer Bill Koch was the first to achieve a notable result on waxless skis in international racing. In the 1976 Winter Olympics, where Koch won a silver medal in the 30-km event on waxable racing skis, he also ran fastest of the skiers of all teams on the third lap of the four-man, 40-km relay race, on waxless skis, a modified pair of Fischer racing skis. The modification was a rectangular patch of mohair under the foot, extending the full width of the ski, and extending about 40 cm (16 in.) in length along the base. The conditions for the race were marginal freezing, difficult for waxing. Koch had selected the mohair skis in preference to waxed skis that seemed to have equal grip.

Koch's result, essentially a first place in an Olympic race, encouraged waxless-ski makers to develop racing models. In the years that followed, top placings (including a few reported wins) in citizens' races were made

midpoint, to give the skier grip. The racing ski requires more force to produce the same midsection pressure and has correspondingly less midsection pressure when lightly weighted, as during a glide on equally weighted skis. This is why racing skis more closely suit the racer's goal of highest possible ski speed. Skis with stiffer midsections are faster because the "slower" grip wax is "up" off the snow during the gliding phases of cross-country strides and contacts the snow only during a forceful, downward kick.

Cambers for racing

A ski's camber stiffness determines the pressure pattern it exerts on the snow as the result of an applied force.

Camber stiffness is determined primarily by the elasticities and stiffnesses of the materials in the ski's structural layers, and by the locations of these layers in the ski. Core materials play a lesser role in overall ski camber stiffness.

Modern ski structural layer materials, such as glass, carbon, and aramid fibers, allow ski makers to produce skis with camber

---

on waxless racing skis. But in international racing, there seemed to be no repeats of Koch's feat. There could have been several reasons: racer resistance, an FIS (International Ski Federation) ruling stipulating that equipment used in FIS-sanctioned races must be commercially available prior to the event, an amazing lack at major meets of the type of transition snow conditions where waxless bases potentially do their best. But in the 1979 Holmenkollen 50 km, the last of the season's World Cup races, the conditions were discouragingly transition, and one racer, like Koch three years earlier, carefully test-skied waxable and waxless bases and settled on the waxless for the race. It paid off: Norwegian racer Per Knut Aaland finished second, 2½ minutes behind winning teammate Oddvar Braa, a result that boosted him to eighth place in the final World Cup standings. Aaland's skis were a pair of Fischer "Racing Crown" waxless skis, with a 90-cm (3-ft.) long "Crown Cut" pattern in the center of the base, shortened 10 cm (4 in.) at each end with paraffin wax filled into the pattern. The tips and tails of Aaland's skis were glide-waxed with paraffin glider wax, as were the waxable skis used in the race by other racers. The 70-cm effective-grip section was sprayed with silicone spray to hinder icing.

Koch was chronologically the first to race on waxless skis and do well (the U.S. team placed sixth, so he won no medal for the feat) in a major race. Aaland was the first to race on commercially available waxless skis and win a medal in a FIS-sanctioned 50 km.

stiffnesses not possible with all-wood ski constructions. This is the basic reason why modern cross-country racing skis are faster than their wood ski predecessors.

The newer ski camber stiffnesses differ from those of wood racing skis in that *the center section is stiffer than the tip and tail sections.* This means that proportionately more force is required to flatten out the center section than is required to flatten out the tip and tail sections of the camber curve. When a ski is weighted, this characteristic distributes more pressure under tip and tail and less under the center of the ski, an effect sometimes termed *double camber.* A ski has only *one* camber, which becomes increasingly stiff as it flattens out. The ideal performance is for ski tips and tails to put pressure on the snow during glide on one or two skis, while center sections put full pressure on the snow only during kicks. In this characteristic lies the advantage of modern ski constructions: first, ski tips and tails are waxed for optimum glide and center sections for optimum grip; second, low center-section pressure during glide wears wax less than if the center were more fully in contact with the snow. How well the performance of a ski approaches this ideal is determined by how well the camber stiffness matches the style and power of the racer and how well it meets the various requirements of snow conditions and tracks. Snow and track conditions can be divided into two categories: wet or dry.

Wet snow tracks are usually fairly firm and sometimes are extremely hard if recently packed by machine. Ski grip is usually good, but glide can be slowed if klister drags during glide. Skis should be relatively stiff, to keep center sections off the snow during glide and to take maximum advantage of the difference between grip and glide waxing.

Dry snow tracks may be firm, but dry snow can compress slightly under the weight of a ski. The overall general effect is that dry snow tracks tend to be slightly softer than wet snow tracks. Glide is a problem only at very low temperatures, but grip sometimes may be difficult. Skis should therefore have a longer grip-waxed section and a shorter glide-waxed section than equivalent skis for wet-snow tracks. Also, as most cross-country grip waxes have fair glide, the transition between grip and glide need not be as marked (or as "sharp") as for wet-snow skis. Therefore, dry-snow skis are less stiff (or "softer") than wet-snow skis for the same racer.

The performances of skis with camber stiffnesses to suit these two conditions, wet and dry, differ in the way the skis apply pressure to the underlying snow during kick, glide on one ski, and glide on two skis:

Kick: Force of three times skier weight or more. Less mid-ski stiffness results in greater mid-ski pressure for dry-snow ski, as required for grip. Pressure over grip section of wet-snow ski is less, more uniform, for even klister wear.

Glide on one ski: Force equal to body weight. Greater mid-ski stiffness results in less mid-ski pressure for wet-snow ski, to reduce klister drag.

Glide on two skis: Force equal to half body weight. Greater mid-ski stiffness keeps center of wet-snow ski off snow to minimize klister drag. More uniform tip and tail pressure exerted under dry-snow ski, for best glide in cold snow.

This means that, for best results, racers should have at least two pairs of skis, with different characteristics: *Dry-snow skis*—Softer; longer mid-ski grip-waxed section. *Wet-snow skis*—Stiffer; more abrupt difference between grip and glide; shorter mid-ski grip-waxed section.

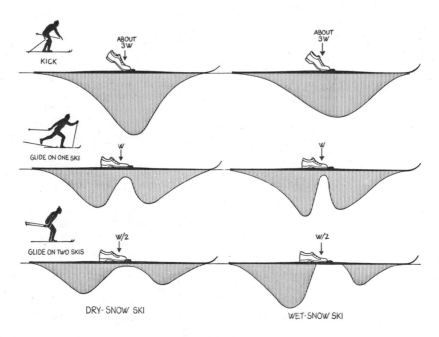

Ideally, the pressure distributions under wet-snow and dry-snow skis differ.

83

Camber stiffnesses are, of course, relative to skier weight and proficiency. Most racers can use the same model of ski, in two different stiffnesses, for their dry-snow and wet-snow skis. Some manufacturers have gone a step further and offer special models of dry-snow and wet-snow skis, primarily as a service to national-team racers and other top competitors. Wet-snow versions of these skis can differ from dry-snow versions in two ways. First, the transition between the softer tip and tail and the stiffer center of the camber is more pronounced, achieved in production either by increased spacing and/or curvature of the upper and lower structural layers, or by additional mid-ski structural layers. Second, the wet-snow versions may have lower-density polyethylene bases, often factory-saturated with paraffin wax for best glide on wet snow.

Racer fitness is also important in selecting camber stiffness. Most racers can kick strongly for the duration of shorter races but

WHAT IT TAKES TO WIN

There's one unending argument in cross-country ski racing: who are the best racers, those of today or those of the past? All agree that modern cross-country ski races are run faster than ever. But, the old-timers rightfully point out, the past champs of the sport skied with heavier gear on slower tracks; what if . . .

So the discussion of the hypothetical race that never can be goes on, as neither past tracks nor past champs still in their prime are available for testing on today's racing scene. But equipment, particularly skis, can be compared, and here lies part of the story of the development of cross-country ski racing, from the first special cross-country racing ski of 1915, to the apex of wood-based wood cross-country racing skis of 1968, to the synthetic-fiber racing skis of today.

Three Typical Winners of Their Time

Year, ski	Construction	Length, cm Imprinted	Chord	Widths, mm, shoulder, waist, heel	Weight, kg (lb, oz)
1915 Bergendahl	Hickory	—	222	67.8, 54.4, 58.5	3.6 kg (7 lb. 15 oz.)
1968 Blå-Skia	Laminated woods, birch base	210	206.7	53.8, 46.5, 52.0	1.5 kg (3 lb. 5 oz.)
1979 Karhu	Kevlar fiber, polyethylene base	210	204.3	43.6, 44.0, 44.0	1.3 kg (2 lb. 14 oz.)

gradually tire, and thus lose kick power, toward the end of longer events. Therefore, stiff skis that grip well at the start of a long race may slip later on, as the racer tires and cannot apply enough kick force for grip. Consequently, racers often select softer skis for longer races (50 km for men and 20 km for women) than they would for shorter races with the same snow conditions.

Many ski makers now measure and imprint stiffnesses on racing skis, usually expressed as numbers or letters, related by charts to body weight. These charts are devised for average racers; strong racers should select skis stiffer than indicated by the charts, and less proficient racers should select skis softer than indicated.

Racers who cannot afford two or more pairs of competition skis should select a pair that matches the most prevalent snow conditions where they race, or a pair that is a compromise between dry-snow and wet-snow ski cambers.

4   BOOT-BINDING SYSTEMS

Cross-country ski boots attach by the toes of their soles to bindings, which are mounted on skis: the connection allows skier control of skis.

Boots and bindings are the only two items of ski equipment that must mate and work together. Boots were once made in a wide variety of sole widths, profiles, and thicknesses, varying by make, model, and size of boot. Therefore, cross-country toe bindings were made adjustable, so as to better fit as many boots as possible. This system had many disadvantages. First, if the bindings were of the type that could be adjusted after being mounted on the skis, they were unduly heavy and their adjustment mechanisms were subject to damage. If they were of the type that was adjusted to fit the boots and then mounted, thereafter being unadjustable, they fitted only one type, and often only one pair, of boots. Second, adjustable bindings had to be mounted with many screws, sometimes as many as five to seven, which often weakened skis.

Fortunately, these disadvantages have almost completely disappeared, as almost all cross-country ski boots and bindings are now made according to one of three boot-binding systems, each of which assures precise boot-binding mate.

Oldest and most prevalent of the systems is the *Nordic Norm,* an outgrowth of the original *Rottefella* system (trade name, patented in 1928). The Nordic Norm system specifies binding and boot-sole side angles and three standard widths, 71 mm, 75 mm, and 79 mm, as measured on the *transverse line,* a line through the outer two pins of a binding or pin recesses in a boot sole. Most common is the

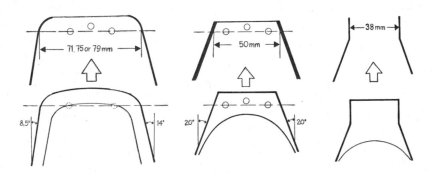

The three boot-binding standards: Nordic Norm, Racing Norm, and Norm 38.

75-mm width, and almost all light-touring boots, now most popular in recreational cross-country skiing, come in this width. The soles on Nordic Norm boots are 12 mm (slightly less than ½ in.) thick, and bindings are designed accordingly. Side angles of binding toepieces and the portion of boot soles fitting into bindings are standardized at 8.5° inner and 14° outer, so a right boot fits only a right binding and a left boot fits only a left binding. Attachment is by a bail or spring-loaded mechanism that holds the boot sole in such a way that pins in the binding mate with recesses in the boot, or binding spikes go through holes in the boot sole.

Nordic Norm boots and bindings were developed in the late 1960s, and by the early 1970s they were the only types available. They are made in a variety of models, suited to uses from racing to

SKIS WITH WITH BINDINGS, OR WHAT'S IN A NAME?

He was a racer and he had just perfected his invention, a new ski binding that was stronger, easier to get into and out of, and worked better than any on the market. It should have a name, he thought. Perhaps it should be named after its inventor, as was then the custom. But he was a modest man, and he also knew that not all names would be good for bindings. Sir Arnold Lunn, later to be the originator of slalom racing and hence of Alpine ski racing, had written in his manual *Ski-ing* that "the Huitfeldt binding with the Höyer-Ellefsen strap clamp is undoubtedly the most used binding in Norway and on the Continent." And that was a mouthful. Too much.

The problem was soon solved, when he entered a race wearing his new bindings. Officiating at the race, the crown prince, himself an avid competitor, saw the new bindings and asked what they were. "Oh!" stammered the inventor-racer, unaccustomed to speaking with royalty, "they're just a pair of rat traps that I bought at the hardware store." The crown prince laughed and told others. The inventor-racer finished well, so well that other racers wanted his "rat traps." Five other racers got pairs, and successfully used them to win the military patrol event in the Winter Olympics, held in St. Moritz, Switzerland, a month later.

The year was 1928; the country was Norway. The inquisitive crown prince was Olav, now King Olav V. The inventor-racer with the new binding was Bror With, so maybe if he had named the binding after himself, today's ad writers in English-speaking countries would have had a field day: "Get with it in Withs, . . . Skis with With bindings . . . ." But the name "Rat trap" stuck. And "rat trap" in Norwegian is "Rottefella," a trade name now synonymous with the pin-type toe binding.

By this measure, perhaps today's racing bindings should be called "mouse traps?"

ski mountaineering. As racing skis and boots slimmed through the years, the Nordic Norm profiles and widths became cumbersome by comparison. Starting in the mid-1970s, two new boot-binding systems were developed for racing: the *Norm 38* and the *Racing Norm 50 mm* systems.

In both systems, a forward extension ("snout") on the boot sole fits into the binding. Boot-sole snouts and bindings are symmetrical, so there's no right or left ski, and boot soles are thinner than for the Nordic Norm system boots, only 7 mm (slightly more than ¼ in.) thick. Both have the advantages of offering a lighter, more flexible boot-binding system than possible with a Nordic Norm design. Lower weight gives racers less to carry, and greater flexibility means that they expend less energy in bending boot soles forward, both of which leave more racer energy available for skiing speed.

Historically, the Norm 38 system was first, being developed prior to and used in the 1976 Winter Olympic cross-country events in Seefeld, Austria. In the Norm 38 system, the boot-sole snout is rectangular, 38 mm (about 1½ in.) wide, and fits into a binding toepiece of corresponding shape. Attachment is either by a pin

---

ISO!

Starting in 1980, you may find cross-country ski boots and bindings marked "ISO." Contrary to the way it sounds when pronounced, *ISO* isn't the transliteration of a Japanese epithet, but rather the initials of the very serious International Standards Organization. The *ISO* marking on a boot or binding indicates the manufacturer's compliance with the ISO design standards, devised to assure product uniformity. The goal is that boots and bindings made according to the standards will mate, regardless of manufacturer, model, or country of origin. New in 1979, the ISO cross-country boot and binding standards are based on those of common boot-binding systems now in use, as shown in the table below. Manufacturers may indicate compliance with ISO standards by marking products with relevant standard number.

ISO Standards		Supplants present standard for boots and bindings
Boots	**Bindings**	
ISO 4711 Nordic 71	ISO 4713 Nordic 71	Nordic Norm 71 mm
ISO 4711 Nordic 75	ISO 4713 Nordic 75	Nordic Norm 75 mm
ISO 4711 Nordic 79	ISO 4713 Nordic 79	Nordic Norm 79 mm
ISO 4712 Racing	ISO 4714 Racing	Racing Norm 50 mm
ISO 4712 Touring	ISO 4714 Touring	Touring Norm 50 mm

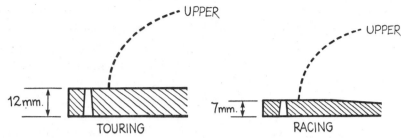

Sole thicknesses also differ: 12 mm for Nordic Norm and Touring Norm (left), 7 mm for Norm 38 and Racing Norm (right).

inserted from one side to the other through the snout piece, or by a clamp that pulls the snout piece forward into the binding.

The Racing Norm 50 mm system resembles its predecessor, the Nordic Norm. Boot sole snouts and binding ears are at a 20° angle, and the 50-mm width is measured on the transverse line through the outer two binding pins or boot sole recesses. Attachment mechanisms are similar to those used in the Nordic Norm system.

The advantages of the newer boot-binding systems—lighter weight, greater freedom for forward foot flex, and lack of right or left on skis—made them rapidly popular among skilled cross-country recreational skiers. But in recreational skiing, two disadvantages immediately became obvious. First, the thinner boot soles were poorer insulators than their Nordic Norm counterparts: the boots were colder. Second, the sole material, a hard plastic, was slippery underfoot when walking. A recent hybrid that solves these problems is the *Touring Norm 50 mm* system, in which boots and bindings have Racing Norm 50 mm profiles, but boots have 12 mm soles and bindings are designed accordingly.

5 BOOTS

Boots for cross-country skiing come in a spectrum of designs and are made of a wide variety of materials, as suits their different purposes. Generally speaking, cross-country ski boots are utilitarian footwear, like running or jogging shoes or hiking boots. Boots are perhaps the most critical item of ski equipment: they are personal, they should fit *you. Be kind to your feet* is the first maxim.

PHYSICAL CHARACTERISTICS

Length in ski boots is indicated by size numbers, according to European, English, or U.S. shoe-size systems. European boots usually are sized according to the *Paris Point System,* in which sizes are 1.5 times the inside length of a shoe or boot. For example, a boot with an inside length of 28 cm (about 13¼ in.) is a size 42.

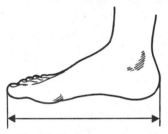

European boot sizes are related to bare foot length.

Each whole number increase in size corresponds to ⅔ cm increase in inside length. Some European boots, especially those made by larger athletic shoe makers, are sized in both the English and the European systems. U.S. and English sizes are not as conveniently

BOOT SIZE COMPARISON TABLE

Scale	Values
CM.	8 9 10 11 12 13 14 15 16 17 18 19 20 21 22 23 24 25 26 27 28 29 30 31 32
EUROPEAN SIZES	12 13 14 15 16 17 18 19 20 21 22 23 24 25 26 27 28 29 30 31 32 33 34 35 36 37 38 39 40 41 42 43 44 45 46 47 48
ENGLISH SIZES	0 1 2 3 4 5 6 7 8 9 10 11 12 13 1 2 3 4 5 6 7 8 9 10 11 12 13
U.S. MEN'S SIZES	0 1 2 3 4 5 6 7 8 9 10 11 12 13 1 2 3 4 5 6 7 8 9 10 11 12 13
U.S. WOMEN'S SIZES	1 2 3 4 5 6 7 8 9 10 11 12 13

related to length as European sizes: whole-size-number size differences correspond to ⅓ inch, with women's size numberings starting at a length of slightly more than eight inches, and men's size numberings starting at a length of about 8¾ inches. Size systems are compared in the size table.

Boots should be chosen about 1.5 cm ($^{19}/_{32}$ in.) longer than feet to provide clearance for socks and forward toe movement when the foot is flexed in skiing or walking. Therefore, to find approximate European sizes from bare foot lengths in centimeters (length in inches times 2.54), add 1.5 cm and then multiply by 1.5.

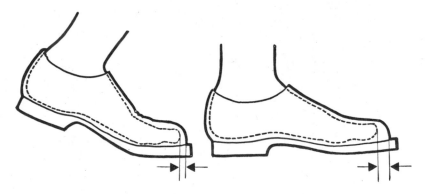

Feet move forward when boot flexes, which cuts toe room.

Width in ski boots, which are usually worn with one or more pairs of relatively heavy socks, is not as critical as in more snugly fitting street shoes. Therefore, most ski boot makers offer only one or two widths in each size, based on average foot-plus-sock lasts. Widths and lengths are not always equal for different models of boots of the same numbered size, because different lasts or differing production techniques may be used. In general, the inside boot circumference at the ball of the foot around the instep and sole increases 4.5 mm (about $^3/_{16}$ in.) for each whole-number increase in European size number.

Sole widths and side angles now follow one of the three standards, Nordic Norm, Norm 38 or Racing Norm, described in Chapter 4.

Height is seldom stated as a measurement but usually is implied by the cut of a boot for racing (below the ankle, like a track shoe), light-touring (at the ankle, like jogging shoes), touring, or mountaineering (above the ankle, like hiking boots).

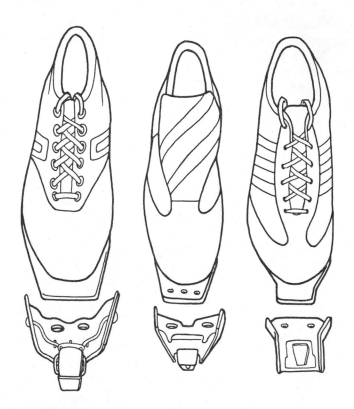

Boots match bindings, according to (from left) Nordic Norm, Racing Norm, or Norm 38 systems.

Weight is sometimes stated in consumer data for boots, and is usual catalog information. A prevalent specification is weight per boot: one speaks, for instance, of a "340-gram shoe" (12 ounces) for a pair weighing 680 grams (1 pound 8 ounces). If not so specified, weight is often for a pair. If sizes are not stated, weights are usually for men's size 8½.

Flexibility is an indication of the ease with which a foot can bend forward unhindered when in a boot. High flexibility means that little energy is expended to bend the boot forward. Low flexibility means that the skier expends effort to overcome sole stiffness underfoot. Although strictly a property of boots and bindings working together, flexibility is primarily determined by overall boot sole flex. Boot sole materials should not only flex easily, but should retain their flex properties at low temperatures. Many materials used in conventional shoe soles or in the soles of athletic shoes

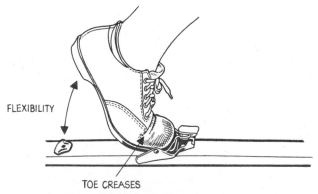

FLEXIBILITY

TOE CREASES

Flexibility is an indication of forward foot freedom.

intended for warm weather sports are unsuitable for ski boot soles because they become stiff as temperature drops.

Lateral stability describes how a weighted but otherwise unrestrained boot heel stays on a ski when the boot toe is clamped in a binding. It is chiefly determined by boot shank stiffness, but is actually meaningful only for the actual use conditions of boots in bindings that are mounted on skis. Lateral stability is sometimes called *control,* because boots with good lateral stability resist sideways heel movement and thus afford good ski control.

Waterproofness applies to complete boots but usually is measured only for upper materials. Waterproofness is measured in a *Bally Penetrometer,* in which upper leather is stretched on a frame that moves from side to side in front of a stream of water. If it takes four hours or more for the water to penetrate through to the opposite side, the leather is termed "waterproof." This means that even "waterproof" leather uppers may let water in after four hours'

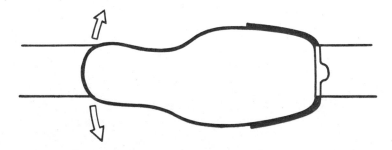

Lateral stability is an indication of how well a weighted boot heel stays on a ski.

use in wet conditions. Synthetics can be more impervious for longer periods of time but do not "breathe" as well as leather: foot moisture is trapped inside the boot.

Toe creases occur in all shoes. Boot design aims at placing toe creases where they neither hinder boot movement in the binding nor rub against the foot.

CONSTRUCTION AND MATERIALS

Aside from being classified according to sole profile standard and intended skiing use, cross-country ski boots are classified according to the manner in which the soles are fastened to the uppers.

Until the mid 1960s, most ski-boot makers used the Norwegian welt construction in which boot uppers are sewn to laminated leather or leather-rubber sandwich soles. However, almost all boots now have molded soles; the Norwegian sewn welt construction is used mostly for heavier touring and ski mountaineering boots. There are three major methods of fastening molded soles to boot uppers: cementing, vulcanizing, and injecting. All three start with a complete but otherwise soleless boot, with uppers sewn or glued to insoles.

Cemented construction means that complete molded rubber or plastic soles are bonded to boot uppers with an adhesive, in a heat and pressure process that may have one or two stages. This is the oldest method of fastening molded soles to boot uppers; it offers the

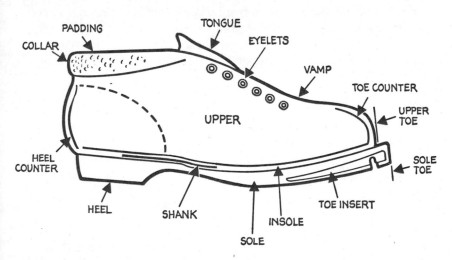

The anatomy of a typical cross-country boot.

bootmaker the greatest flexibility of production model changes and allows soles and sole-to-upper bonds to be inspected and checked at several stages in the production process.

Vulcanized soles are made on the boots. Boot uppers are placed on top of a mold that contains a raw rubber blank of the correct size to form the sole. Then pressure is applied and the mold is raised to vulcanization temperature, 160°C (320°F). After six to eight minutes, vulcanization is complete, the mold is cooled, and the finished boot is removed. Only natural rubber or styrene butadiene (SB), a synthetic rubber, may be used for vulcanized soles. Vulcanized soles retain their flexing properties well at low temperatures.

Injected soles are made in a manner similar to that for vulcanized soles. Finished uppers are placed on top of a mold, into which liquid sole material is injected under pressure and heat and then allowed to harden. The process may have many steps, all dependent on the technology of the particular material used.

Most injected soles are made of either thermoplastic rubber (TR) or polyurethane (PU) foam. Polyvinylchloride (PVC) foam, which is less expensive than TR or PU, has also been used. Injected compact polyamide soles are used on racing and some light-touring boots.

TR is a synthetic rubber that melts at about 155°C (311°F). In its molten state, TR is injected into the sole mold and then allowed to cool.

PU injection involves a chemical process. Its two constituents are rapidly mixed and injected into the sole mold. Carbon dioxide evolves during the ensuing reaction, filling the material with small bubbles. After three to four minutes, the polyurethane is cured and the soles are finished. Injected PU foam bonds well to uppers, so the process is used for a wide variety of sports shoes, from cross-country ski boots to jogging shoes. Polyamides, such as Hytrel®, a type of nylon, can be injected. The process involved resembles that used to make injected soles on soccer shoes and results in a hard, thin (7 mm, about ¼ in. thick) sole.

Sole properties can be altered both by compounding with other materials and by controlling the degree of expansion, or how much the plastic foams during hardening. This allows the boot designer freedom to make special soles.

In terms of characteristics and cost, there are no decisive fundamental differences between the three methods of attaching molded boot soles to boot uppers. In theory, the cemented sole process is potentially the least expensive for the bootmaker, as soles are

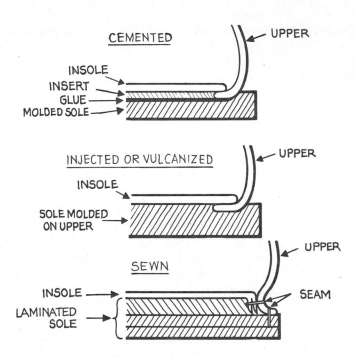

Three basic sole-to-upper boot constructions.

simply purchased and glued to uppers. However, the adhesive used may be expensive and the bonding techniques as time consuming as vulcanization or injection molding, so for boots of similar quality there may be little or no cost advantages over other systems. In principle, vulcanized or injected sole boots are potentially more waterproof than cemented-sole boots, as the sole material impregnates the pores of the upper material and seals out water. But differences in finished boot soles or in the quality of their bond to boot uppers are more due to material qualities and properties and to the bootmaker's skill and quality control than to any technical advantage of a process.

Most molded soles have toe insert plates or reinforcements, with holes, eyelets, or grooves designed to fit the mechanisms of the corresponding bindings involved. These insert plates are made of steel, aluminum alloy, or plastic compounds, such as Desmopan, a trade name for a high-strength polyurethane compound.

Molded soles are made of homogeneous materials that are equally flexible in all directions. A good boot sole should allow forward foot flex but prevent twist or sideways movement of the heel with respect to the toe. These desirable characteristics are attained with homogeneous sole materials in a number of ways. First, the top side of the sole, under the boot insole, can be profiled or segmented in a wafflelike pattern that hinges forward, but not sideways. Second, the sole may be stiffened against lateral flex by inserting a steel, plastic, or wood gusset in the boot shank, which is the narrow part of the sole, lying beneath the instep. Third, the sole may be reinforced with or laminated with other materials to achieve the desired flex. Finally, a combination of these methods may be used.

Tongues are usually of the bellows type, that is, sewn to the uppers on both sides under the laces, a feature designed for best water repellency. But snow can collect under exposed laces, melt, and wet through the tongue. Therefore, some models of boots also have a second tongue over the laces, held in place by Velcro tape or a second set of laces. Most tongues are made of the same materials as the boot uppers, but many leather boots now have tongues that are all synthetic, usually polyurethane sandwiched on top of a thin padding layer, for better water repellency.

Padding inside a boot and around the collar softens boot-to-foot contact and reduces chafing. Collar padding also seals the boot around the ankle.

Uppers

As for shoes and other boots, the material used in ski boot uppers is perhaps what most people think of first when classifying a boot—a leather boot, a rubber boot, and so on. Cross-country ski boots are made with leather or synthetic uppers.

Leather boots are those in which the uppers are made of leather and only minor parts such as counters, tongues, collars, and the like may be made of other materials. Most ski boots are leather boots, because leather has the unique ability to breathe yet be waterproof.

All animal hides and skins used in boots are converted to leathers by tanning, which makes them pliable and prevents their becoming hard or rotting. The tanning process varies according to the properties desirable in the final leather. Almost all leathers for uppers are chrome tanned, which involves steeping hide in a bath of chrome salt solution.

Tanned cowhide is the most widely used leather for ski boots. Cowhide is usually classified according to age (calfskin, heifer, cowhide) and condition. Calfskin is usually regarded as best and older cowhide as poorest. The hide of the adult animal is too thick for boot uppers, so it is split into sheets of varying thickness. The outside, or top sheet, is called *top grain*. It is regarded as best for boot uppers because of its tough surface and natural oiliness that resists water and moisture. All other layers are called *split leather*. Less expensive than top grain, split leathers have less natural water repellency and stretch more readily. Split leather has a rough surface that resembles suede but is sometimes given a plastic coating, usually polyurethane or polyvinylchloride, which improves water repellency and gives it the appearance of top grain. Some boots have "rough out" leather uppers, which may be either reversed top grain (smooth side in, rough side out) or a roughened split.

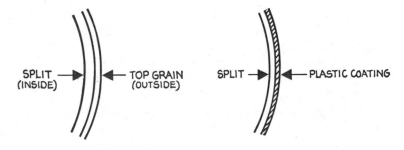

Thick cowhide is split into thinner layers for use in boots. Split leather can be coated to resemble top grain.

Kangaroo skin and goat skin are thin, strong leathers, usually more costly and less water repellent than cowhide. Therefore they are used mostly for ultra-lightweight, more expensive racing boots.

Chrome-tanned leather absorbs water almost as well as blotting paper and must be treated to repel water. The treatments used most involve impregnation with silicone compounds and result in leathers that retain their flexibility under all skiing temperatures.

Several silicone treatments are now in use: all may be classified according to the water-repellent action of the final treated leather: *hydrophilic* or *hydrophobic*.

Hydrophilic leather has a slight affinity for water, so it repels water much as canvas does: the surface fibers absorb water and expand to close the pores to further water penetration.

Hydrophobic leathers are the more water repellent, being able to withstand more than 12 hours testing in the Bally Penetrometer

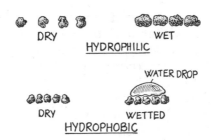

DRY   WET
HYDROPHILIC

WATER DROP

DRY WETTED
HYDROPHOBIC

Hydrophilic leather (top) acts like canvas to repel water: its fibers expand when wet. Hydrophobic leather (bottom) has pores so small that water cannot penetrate.

without wetting through, as compared to four hours for most hydrophilic leathers. But the involved, multistage treatment processes have made these leathers expensive, so they thus far are used mostly in the uppers of competition and other more costly boots.

Some bootmakers use a synthetic coating of polyurethane or PVC for waterproofing and coloring upper leathers. Oil-impregnated leathers are no longer used for ski boots.

Since waterproofed leather is impervious to dyes, final leather coloring must be done before waterproofing. The natural color of chrome-tanned cowhide is a light gray; a good dye will penetrate. There is virtually no technical limitation on the choice of color, except that white and other light colors are regarded as difficult because the waterproofing processes yellow the leather surface slightly.

The only satisfactory method of producing a boot leather that is both white and as waterproof as other colored leathers is to use a more involved dyeing process, usually with two or more stages that include color fixation. This is why white boots are sometimes more expensive than corresponding models in other colors. The alternative is to follow the traditional approach to producing white leathers: reduce or eliminate the waterproofing process, with the result that these white boots are less waterproof than those of other colors.

The thicknesses of leathers used in uppers vary with boot make and model. But most leather uppers on racing and many light touring boots are 1.2 to 1.4 mm (about 3/64 in.) thick, while average light-touring and touring boot uppers use a 2.0-mm (5/64-in.) thickness.

Synthetic boots have uppers with few or no leather parts. The uppers may be made of *textile* or *synthetic leather materials*, similar to those used for the uppers of running and other athletic shoes, where the material is often perforated for ventilation.

Textile uppers are actually multi-layer sandwiches, usually of two fabrics separated by a thin foam plastic layer that pads and insulates. The overall thickness is about 2.5 to 3.0 mm ($^1/_{10}$ to $^1/_8$ in.). The fabrics are usually nylon or polyester-cotton; polypropylene foam is a commonly used padding. Some upper textile materials, such as Soft-Lite®, are coated with a thin outer film of plastic, usually compact polyurethane. These films increase water repellency and aid insulation, but reduce breathability. This can be a drawback for boots used for day-long tours in warmer snow conditions. But for lightweight racing boots, especially for those used at low temperatures, −10°C (14°F) and below, breathability is less important than insulation.

Most boots with textile uppers have leather or synthetic leather toes and heels for abrasion resistance where it is most needed and for a good bond to the sole where the stress between upper and sole is greatest. The textile materials themselves usually bond poorly to soles.

Synthetic leather uppers, such as Cangoran®, are also multilayer sandwiches, usually of four or five different materials. The major differences between the synthetic leather sandwich materials and textile upper sandwich materials is that the fibers of the synthetic leathers are not woven, but lie in all directions, as in leather, and the overall sandwich is denser and stronger. Most synthetic leathers breathe less well than natural leather.

Textile and synthetic leather uppers are now available in most makes of racing boots and in many makes of light-touring and touring boots. Some bootmakers contend that these materials may eventually dominate, because they allow boots to be made lighter and in a wider range of colors than possible with leather uppers, and because quality leathers are becoming increasingly expensive.

The disadvantage of synthetic uppers is that if they breathe as well as leather, they are less waterproof. However, once wet, they dry more quickly than leather boots.

Some boots have rubber, synthetic rubber, or PVC uppers that are completely waterproof, like galoshes. These boots are preferred by skiers who continually ski in slush. As they do not breathe at all, they usually are lined with synthetic pile fleece to absorb foot moisture.

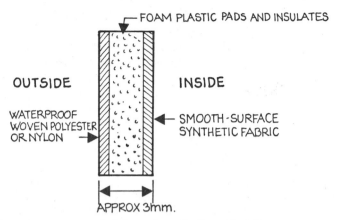

FOAM PLASTIC PADS AND INSULATES

OUTSIDE

INSIDE

WATERPROOF
WOVEN POLYESTER
OR NYLON

SMOOTH-SURFACE
SYNTHETIC FABRIC

APPROX 3mm.

Textile uppers are sandwiches of synthetic materials.

Miscellaneous parts

Lining for warmth inside boots has traditionally been made of fur or wool fleece, but now most linings are made of synthetics such as nylon or polyester. Linings are made in so many different weaves and piles that type classification isn't practical, except that nylon pile is regarded as the most elastic and most durable.

In general, lined boots take longer to dry and retain foot odors longer than unlined or leather-lined boots. The choice between pile-lined boots and slightly roomier unlined boots with space enough for extra socks then depends on how often the boots are used and the available drying facilities.

Insoles are made of tanned leather, leather fiber, or cellulose fiber. Good insoles are light in weight, able to absorb perspiration, durable, and provide air circulation. They should also be stiff enough to stabilize the boot during manufacture and in use and provide a good bond to the sole.

Thread: Classic bootmaking practice called for the use of silk, linen, or cotton thread, but today's ski boots use nylon or polyester thread in all seams.

BOOT TYPES

Boots classified into the four skiing categories according to intended use differ primarily in cut, or boot height at the ankle. Boots in the racing end of the spectrum are cut low, which minimizes boot weight and maximizes foot freedom. Boots in the touring end of the spectrum are cut high for increased warmth and ankle support.

Racing boots resemble running or jogging shoes but differ in that they have soles designed to fit bindings on skis and are usually made on slightly larger lasts that allow for the greater thickness of winter ski socks. They also are usually better insulated than jogging shoes, as suits their cold-weather use. But the weights of the two types of footwear are about the same, approximately 680 grams (1½ pounds) a pair, for men's size 10 cross-country ski racing boots or all-around jogging shoes.

Racing boots now have relatively thin (7 mm, slightly less than ¼ in.) soles of hard plastic, usually a polyamide material such as Hytrel®, or of a polyurethane. Soles are made with front extensions, or "snouts," to fit Norm 38 or Racing Norm 50 bindings, and uppers are made of top-quality leathers, synthetic leather, or textile. The hard soles are slippery underfoot for walking, so some bootmakers insert rubber toe and/or heel pads for better grip. In skiing, the rubber heels help absorb the shock when boot heels meet skis, a feature many racers appreciate: a "softer" underfoot feeling. Heels are designed with a rubber pad to mate either against a peg or serrated surface in a heel plate, or with a groove that mates against a wedge mounted on the ski. All racing boots have eyelet lacing and most have bellows tongues. Some models feature a second waterproofing tongue to cover the laces, held in place with Velcro tape. Most racing boots are unlined or leather lined.

Light-touring boots are cut slightly higher than racing boots and often have grooves around the outside of the heel for use with cable bindings. Uppers are made of top grain, coated split, or sueded leather, or of nylon textile or other synthetics. Most light-touring boot soles are molded, but some models have sewn soles. Most light-touring boot soles now have Nordic Norm profiles and thickness, but Norm 38 and Touring Norm 50 light-touring boots are available. Eyelet lacing is the most common, but some boots feature partial ring, full ring, or hook speed lacing. Most tongues are of the bellows type, but some heavier light-touring boots have lap tongues. Many bootmakers offer corresponding lined and unlined models. All synthetic-upper boots are lined to compensate for the poorer insulating and moisture absorption properties of synthetics.

Touring and mountain boots are cut above the ankle and resemble hiking boots. Uppers are made of leather, in almost all its available varieties, or of synthetics. Most soles are molded, but heavier ski mountaineering boots, especially those with lug soles such as Vibram®, have Norwegian welts. Almost all touring and ski mountaineering boots have Nordic Norm profiles and sole thicknesses, although some heavier ski mountaineering boots have thicker soles and non-norm side profiles. Double lacing is often used; the inner laces run through eyelets over a bellows tongue, and the outer laces run through rings or hooks over a hinged tongue. Most boot makers offer both lined and unlined models, although lined are now the most popular. Most models are padded, usually around the entire ankle and up to the collar. The heels have grooves for cable bindings.

Children's boots are usually smaller versions of touring boots. **Junior** boots are simply smaller sizes of the corresponding boots for adults.

6 BINDINGS

PHYSICAL CHARACTERISTICS

Width is usually the only dimension imprinted on a binding or printed on its packaging. Width is measured on the transverse line, which

—for Nordic Norm, Racing Norm, and Touring Norm bindings goes through the centers of the outer pins of a pin-type binding, and

—for Norm 38 bindings is in the forward part of the toepiece, where the edges are parallel.

The standard Nordic Norm binding widths are 71 mm, 75 mm, and 79 mm. Some models are available in an 83-mm width to fit extra-large boots. These widths have often been designated by names—such as extra small, small, wide, and extra wide—but without uniformity among manufacturers. Therefore, current Nordic Norm standard bindings have widths stipulated in millimeters only: the most common width is now 75 mm. The standard Racing Norm and Touring Norm width is 50 mm. The standard Norm 38 width is 38 mm.

Weight is pair weight *with screws.*

Screw hole sizes and location are now standard. Bindings are mounted with three screws, one forward and two back. The center of the forward screw is located 47 mm ($1^{27}/_{32}$ in.) ahead of the center

---

SKIING SPIN-OFF

A technological spin-off involves the application of something developed for another purpose, usually by a different industry. The aerospace industry is noted for its spin-offs that benefit other industries: many of the materials now used in ski equipment and apparel were originally developed for aerospace applications. A reverse of the process occurs seldom: skiing is so specialized that its technology has few applications elsewhere. But there's one recent exception to this rule that may revolutionize part of the equipment of another sport: rowing.

Traditionally, rowers and scullers brace their feet against a cross strut, called a *stretcher,* in their shells. Secure foot bracing has been assured by screwing boots to stretchers. This fixing of boots to boat has several disadvantages. First, there's potential danger: rowers can be trapped in capsized boats, unless they have special quick-release devices on their boots. Second, boots are always as wet as the interior of the shell: it's uncomfortable to always get into wet boots. Finally, boots may only fit one set of feet in a crew, making changes difficult.

line of the rear two screws. For Nordic Norm bindings, the rear screws may be located with centers spaced 32 mm (1¼ in.) or 26 mm (1¹/₆₄ in.) from each other. The wider spacing, 32 mm, is usually intended for bindings to be mounted on wider, heavier touring skis, while the closer spacing, 26 mm, is intended for bindings to be mounted on most light-touring skis. The rear screw center spacing for all Racing Norm, Touring Norm, and Norm 38 bindings is 26 mm. All screw holes should accept 9 mm head diameter, 90° countersink screws. Deviations from these standard screw locations are

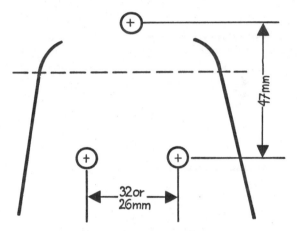

Screw locations are now standardized.

This situation, thought athletic shoemaker Adidas, was about as logical as screwing cross-country ski boots to skis. So Adidas used the old, reliable boot-in-toe-binding principle to develop the Aviron® rowing shoe and binding. Aviron® bindings resemble a set of spike-type Nordic Norm bindings mounted on a single plastic plate, with swivels in the middle of each toepiece so feet may pivot. Aviron® boots resemble Nordic Norm cross-country racing boots, except that their uppers are made of lighter, perforated material to cut water absorption to a minimum. The bindings are fitted with large, red quick-release catches, similar to those on step-in cross-country ski bindings, for rapid release in case of boat capsize. Bindings are mounted on shell stretchers; oarsmen can now walk to and from their shells wearing their own boots. First fully tested at the 1979 World Championships in New Zealand and the 1979 International Regatta in Lucerne, Switzerland, the system was rapidly accepted.

For once, a cross-country spin-off . . .

found in a few nonstandard bindings and in some heavier bindings for ski mountaineering.

Side angles on toe bindings are standardized according to the various standards described in Chapter 4. These angles apply to the entire area where the edges of the boot sole are in contact with the binding.

Flexibility is a qualitative indication of forward boot movement freedom in a binding mounted on a ski, and thus should not be considered a property of bindings alone.

Lateral stability indicates how well a binding on a ski prevents sideways boot motion. It is a meaningful term only for the actual use conditions of boots in bindings that are mounted on skis.

Stability is a qualitative indication of the foot-to-snow control afforded by the entire boot-binding-ski combination. In most cases, stability can be regarded as meaning control.

Durability for bindings usually refers to the longevity of the various binding parts in actual skiing use.

CONSTRUCTION AND MATERIALS

All bindings comprise two major parts: a toepiece, which holds the boot and is screwed to the ski; and an attachment device for holding the boot in the toepiece. *Toe bindings* combine the toepiece and attachment device in a single unit; the boot is held by clamping the front of its sole. *Cable bindings* use either a cable or a metal strap around the boot heel to press the boot forward into the toepiece.

Through the years, many materials—wood, leather, willow, metal and plastic—have been used to make ski bindings. Bindings

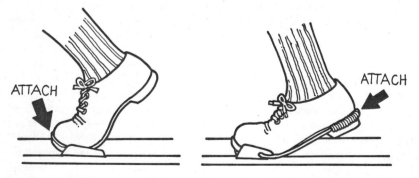

Toe bindings attach at toe of sole only; cable bindings attach by pushing boot forward into toepiece.

are now made entirely of metal or plastic parts, the only exceptions being the textile or leather straps on a few touring and children's bindings. Metal binding parts are stamped, drawn, or forged and machined; plastic parts are injection molded.

Metals

Aluminum is currently the most common metal in ski bindings. "Aircraft aluminum," which is aluminum alloyed with magnesium and manganese, has a high fatigue strength and a high impact strength, even at low temperatures. These properties, combined with its ease of workability in punch presses, make it the most commonly used metal for toepieces. Racing bindings normally use thinner sheets of higher strength aluminum alloys, such as those containing zinc, magnesium, and copper. "Structural aluminum," which is aluminum alloyed with magnesium, silicon, and manganese, has high resistance to wear and is thus used for bails, bail clamps, and various minor binding parts. Most aluminum binding parts are anodized (coated with a protective film by electrochemical means), which can also be used to add surface color.

Steel was once used for toepieces, hence the older designation *toe irons*. Modern bindings use steel only for smaller, stressed parts. *Spring steel wire* is used for bails and for springs on some cable bindings. *Spring steel sheet* is used in some bails, in catch mechanisms of "step-in" bindings, and in pressure mechanisms for through-sole spike attachment devices. *Forged and machined steel* is used for spikes and pins, bail pegs, and various attachment pins. *Steel cable* is used for heel cables.

Plastics

The plastics used in bindings are related to but different from those used in skis. This is chiefly because bindings are rigid, but skis must flex.

Polyacetate (various trademarks, such as Delrin®) and *polyester* (Arnite®) are resins that are injection molded at pressures of 700 to 1000 atmospheres to form toepieces and other major binding parts. These plastics are strong at low temperature and are easily molded. Polyacetate, the stronger of the two, requires higher molding pressure and temperature than polyester. *Polyamid* compounds, such as nylon, are used for binding parts subjected to wear, such as bail hooks. High-stressed polyamid parts are sometimes reinforced with fiberglass.

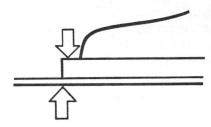

TOE BINDINGS CLAMP BOOT SOLE

WITH A BAIL:

WITH SPIKES:

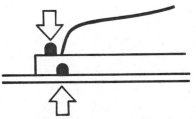

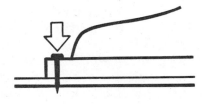

BY PRESSURE AGAINST PINS,

PROJECTING DOWNWARD,

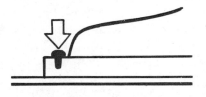

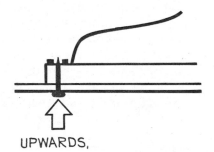

BY PINS IN THE BAIL,

UPWARDS,

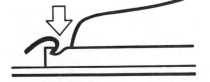

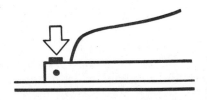

OR WITH A BAIL SPRING CATCH.

OR SIDEWAYS THROUGH THE SOLE.

Toe bindings attach with bails or spikes in various ways.

BINDING TYPES

Toe bindings attach the boot to the ski by clamping the front part of the boot sole into the binding. Most toe bindings have a metal or plastic toepiece and differ from one another only in which part of the sole or its extension is clamped and how the clamping is done. There are two basic types of clamping mechanism: *bails* and *spikes*.

Bails may (1) press the boot sole down against pins in the base-plate of the binding, the oldest and still most common of all binding clamping mechanisms; (2) contain pins that mate with recesses in the top of the boot sole; or (3) themselves be semicircular springs that, when pulled forward, clamp downward, holding a groove in the boot sole, much as a trunk clasp closes.

Spikes may (1) go through eyelets in the sole from the top; (2) go through eyelets in the sole from the bottom, to clamp the sole up against a horizontal part of the toepiece; or (3) go sideways through an extension of the sole to hold the sole wedged between the baseplate and a horizontal member of the toepiece.

Toe bindings allow greater flexibility and are lighter than cable bindings. Cable bindings were once the stronger and more stable and were therefore preferred for wilderness skiing. However, with modern boots, toe bindings are sturdy and stable enough for almost all recreational skiing. In fact, toe bindings are also adequate for skiing in extreme conditions: the 1977 Ellesmere Island expedition

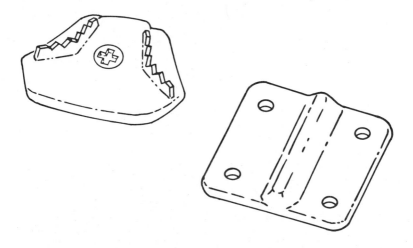

Typical heel plates: serrated metal (left) and wedge (right).

in the Canadian arctic and the 1978 Mt. McKinley circuit ski expedition used toe bindings exclusively.

Heel plates should be mounted on skis to increase boot-binding lateral stability. There are many types of heel plate, but all function to hold a weighted heel on the ski so it does not slide off the ski to the side. Heel plates, or fixtures, fall into two general classes, according to the principle of operation: (1) pins, or metal or plastic edges, sometimes serrated, that dig into a rubber boot heel; or (2) wedges or other shapes that mate with a corresponding groove in the boot heel.

Several heel tie-down and/or so-called boot stabilization devices have been marketed. They either fasten the heel to the ski or guide the heel or rear part of the boot so it cannot be twisted to the side until well off the ski. These devices improve ski control on downhills but also increase the danger of ankle or leg injury in falls, as they defeat part of the foot freedom of boots fixed to toe bindings only.

Cable bindings consist of a heel cable or strap that applies forward pressure on the heel to hold the boot in a toepiece. The toepieces of the various bindings are similar; only the heel straps or cables differ. There are two general types of cable: the heel cable

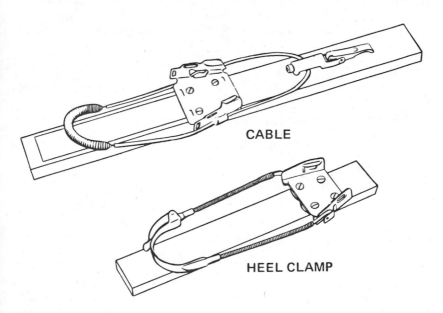

CABLE

HEEL CLAMP

Cable-type bindings.

with a front or rear spring to provide tension, and the heel strap with a ratchet-loaded clamp to provide tension. Both are adjustable. Some models of the front-throw type have accessory hooks mounted on the sides of the ski through which the cable may be run to hold the boot heel down for downhill ski control. This also increases the danger of injury in a fall. Cable-type bindings are heavier than toe bindings but, together with touring boots, can provide better ankle support and a feeling of better ski control. Most cable binding toepieces are now made according to the Nordic Norm standard for toe bindings.

Children's bindings consist of simple toepieces and toe or heel straps of leather or plastic, and are adjustable to suit a wide range of children's winter footwear, including children's ski boots, rubber boots, and snowmobile boots. However, active youngsters of four or five can enjoy skiing more using junior toe bindings and boots.

Use determines type

Bindings are usually classified according to use, but not to the same degree as skis and boots. In general, strength is proportional to weight: lightweight racing bindings are not as strong as those intended for recreational skiing. However, the current trend is toward lighter bindings and boots: types first used in racing in the 1976 Winter Olympics are now used by many recreational skiers.

Racing bindings are made according to the Norm 38 or Racing Norm standards and may be of metal or plastic. Metal racing bindings are usually made of thinner aluminum alloy sheet than recreational bindings, 2.0 mm versus 2.5 mm (0.08 in. versus 0.10 in.). Weights are correspondingly less, about 80 grams (2.8 oz.) per pair versus an average of 140 grams (4.9 oz.) per pair for the lightest Nordic Norm bindings. Attachment devices are usually slightly lighter than the corresponding devices of recreational toe bindings of the same make.

Recreational skiing bindings are now offered in a wide variety of types, made according to all existing boot-binding standard systems. Still most popular are the Nordic Norm standbys, available in a variety of models, ranging from minimum-weight metal or plastic light-touring bindings to sturdier models, intended for wilderness skiing and ski mountaineering. More recently, Norm 38 and Racing Norm bindings have been introduced in models intended for in-track skiing like that done at most cross-country ski areas by recreational skiers on light-touring skis. Touring Norm bindings are now available to suit both light-touring and heavier touring boots. At the heaviest and sturdiest end of the recreational binding spectrum, bindings for wilderness skiing and ski mountaineering, Nordic Norm toe bindings and cable-type bindings are both used.

MOUNTING BINDINGS

Ski, boot, and binding makers agree that the majority of binding faults or ski failures around the binding are caused by improper binding mounting.

Binding mounting is simple and straightforward but, like most other repairs or service operations, is best done with tools and equipment specifically selected for the job. Needed are

- drill, preferably electric,
- 4.0 mm (5/32 in.) and 3.6 mm (9/64 in.) bits, preferably with depth stops,
- binding mounting jig or template,
- T square,
- workbench with a vise,
- center punch,
- hammer,
- screwdriver to fit binding screws, usually Pozi-Drive no. 3,
- marking pen with thin tip.

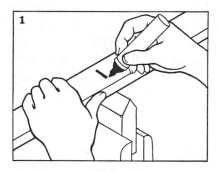 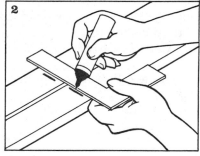

1. Balance ski on a straight edge to find balance line: best is a metal edge clamped in a vise, as shown here. Always check premarked balance points, as locations can vary with positioning of top sheets or silk screening of top cosmetics. Do not find balance line by holding ski between thumb and forefinger or by balancing on a hand-held knife blade, both of which are inaccurate.

2. Compare balance lines for both skis of a pair. If different, take rearmost point as balance for pair. Mark balance line across pair, using a square.

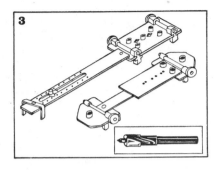

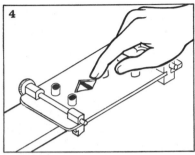

3. Bindings are best mounted using mounting jigs and drills supplied by binding makers. Shown here are two common types of jig, with a special drill bit in the foreground.

4. Locate the binding mounting jig over the balance line marked on the skis. This locates the binding screw holes so the pins of a pin binding are over the ski balance for Nordic Norm boots. For other boots, check upper location with respect to binding screw holes before drilling.

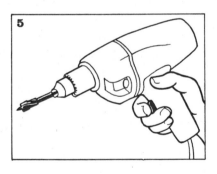

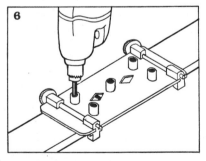

5. Use drill bit with step stop to predrill screw holes. Drill diameter of 4.0 mm ($^5/_{32}$ in.) is most used, but for skis with thinner top laminates, 3.6 mm ($^9/_{64}$ in.) is better. Always check binding maker's instructions for proper bit size.

6. Drill screw holes in ski. As shown here, most jigs have ferrules to guide drill bit.

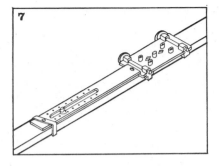

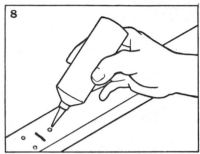

7. *Jigs may be used to locate holes for screw-mounted or pin-type heel plates. When using this accessory, check to see if the heel locator scale is intended for the type of binding and boot being mounted.*

8. *Fill screw holes about half full of glue to bond screws. Recommended glues are Colltana, a special binding screw cement available from Montana Sport, and Elmer's Waterproof glue.*

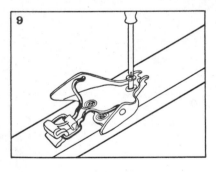

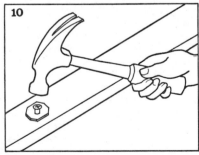

9. *Drive mounting screws. Most bindings now mount with Pozi-Drive no. 3 screws. Keep screwdriver vertical so screws drive true.*

10. *Mount heel plate. Shown here is a pin-type heel plate with the pin driven into the hole located by the binding jig and drilled along with the toepiece holes.*

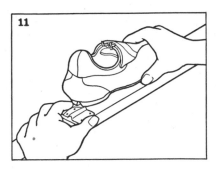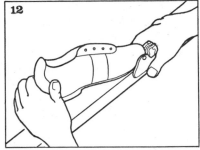

11. Some heel plates, especially those supplied by bootmakers, cannot be located using binding mounting jigs. For these heel plates, locate by fixing boot in binding and locating plate under heel, as shown here for a wedge-type plate, fastened to the ski with self-adhesive and secured with brads.

12. Try boot. Test for heel location on ski and action of boot in binding.

The traditional and still prevalent location for bindings places the front edge of the boot upper at or just slightly behind the ski balance line, as measured without bindings. This location places the force of the kick, which comes approximately from the center of the foot, just at or slightly behind the top of the ski's camber curve, the best location for ski grip. Most recreational skis have fairly gentle camber curves with relatively long top sections, so the "boot toe on the balance line" rule seldom fails to produce good results. But for performance skis, especially stiffer racing skis, binding location may be more critical. For best skiing efficiency, a racer's kick should hit at the top or just behind the top of the camber curve, which may be shorter and more pronounced and located differently than for recreational skis. This is why some racers prefer to mount their bindings farther back, with the fronts of the boot uppers as much as 12 mm (½ in.) behind the ski balance line for most synthetic fiber skis. But this is a personal preference, based on individual skiing style. When in doubt, check the ski manufacturer's data for binding location. In any event, binding mounting starts by finding where the boot will locate relative to the holes to be drilled for the binding mounting screws.

Most bindings now mount with the same spacing between the three mounting screws: 26 mm between the centers of the rear screws and 47 mm from the centerline of the rear screws to the center of the front screw. But the three major binding-boot standards do *not* agree in locations of boot uppers relative to binding mounting screws. The front edge of a boot upper locates behind the center of the front binding mounting screw by

- 22 mm ($^{55}/_{64}$ in.) for Nordic Norm bindings,
- 33 mm ($1^{19}/_{64}$ in.) for Norm 38 bindings, and
- 35 mm (1⅜ in.) for Racing Norm and Touring Norm bindings.

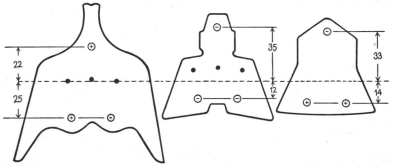

For same location of front of boot upper, shown by dotted line, Nordic Norm (left), Racing Norm (middle), and Norm 38 (right) bindings locate differently on ski.

FOR WANT OF A THREAD

It was the night before the four-man 40-km relay of the 1974 FIS Nordic World Ski Championships, and host country Sweden was favored to win. Seven Swedish racers carefully went over their gear, each preparing to run any one of the relay's four laps. The four to run would be picked just half an hour before the start. The Swedish relay champ, woodsman Hans-Erik Larsson, carefully mounted a pair of pin bindings on a new pair of fiberglass cross-country racing skis, the same make and model that had carried teammate Thomas Magnusson to gold in the 30-km race five days earlier.

At 12:30 on the race day, Sweden's foursome was entered and sprinter Larsson was the first-lap man, a move the Swedish coaches hoped would give the psychological lead necessary to win. The start gun went off as scheduled at 1:00 p.m., and 14 racers surged forward to vie for the lead on two tracks leading out of the stadium just 500 yards away. Larsson gained the lead after 50 yards, and then stumbled and fell as his right ski came off: the binding had pulled straight off the ski. A coach rushed to replace the ski, and Larsson got off just over a minute and a half late.

According to the FIS international ski competition rules, Larsson could now change the right ski as many times as it might again be damaged but had to finish the race on the left ski, the only one remaining of the pair he had started with.

Two kilometers out on the track, Larsson had just caught sight of the

Binding location is simple if jigs or templates designed for the particular binding are used, as they locate the three holes to place the front edge of the boot upper on the ski balance line. But if jigs or templates for another standard are used, the bindings will not be correctly located when mounted. Therefore, always start binding mounting by checking the desired screw location relative to the ski balance line. Then, and only then, adjust for individual preference, such as moving back for some racers.

---

stragglers when his left binding pulled off. A sympathetic East German coach gave him a new left ski, and he was illegally on his way.

Larsson finished the lap just two and a half minutes behind the fastest man, Russian Ivan Garanin, and tagged teammate Sven-Åke Lundbäck for the second lap. But the gamble was unmasked in the routine check made on all racers' skis as they leave the finish area. Larsson had changed both skis and Sweden was disqualified. The Swedish team's walkie-talkies carried the message along the track: stop Lundbäck. For Sweden, who hadn't won an FIS World Ski Championship or Winter Olympic relay in 10 years, it was black Thursday. And the fault lay with six threads, one on each of the six screws Larsson had used to mount his bindings.

For Larsson had mounted the bindings using screws intended for use on wood skis only. The screws lacked sharp threads up to their heads, necessary for bite when driven through fiberglass laminates. Larsson had bonded the screws with adhesive, but the crucial last thread just wasn't there. It was a critical meet, the first major international event in which fiberglass skis won. Many, including Larsson, were unprepared for the switch and were poorly informed on the changes involved. Things are now different, and all binding makers supply bindings with screws that hold both in the thinner synthetic-fiber laminates and in wood.

But at that time the cost was great. For the want of a thread, a race—and the hopes of a country for its team—were lost.

7 POLES

Ski poles often seem relegated to the fringes of the ski equipment picture, as their design, features, and development are seldom the focus of skier attention. Despite this anonymity, the development of modern ski poles has contributed as much to the convenience and ease of cross-country skiing as the development of modern skis has. Ski historians agree that the turning point in ski technique, the start of all forms of modern skiing, occurred in the latter half of the nineteenth century when skiers started using two ski poles instead of the former single pole.

PHYSICAL CHARACTERISTICS

Length is usually the only measurement given for a ski pole. Most pole makers label poles in overall length, from the end of the tip to the end of the grip, although some do not include the tip. Therefore, different makes of pole of the same labeled length may vary in length by as much as 1.5 cm.

Shaft diameter for tonkin shafts is the average of the diameters measured midway between the growth rings. Fiberglass, carbon fiber, and metal shaft diameters are usually measured at the grip end of the shaft. Some tapered shafts are measured at both grip and basket.

Basket diameter is the outer diameter for circular baskets and the largest transverse dimension for noncircular baskets.

Weight is pair weight, with all baskets, straps, etc., mounted.

Balance, or *swing weight,* is a qualitative indication of weight

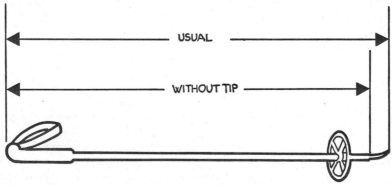

Pole length is usually measured from end to end.

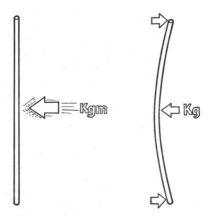

Impact strength (left) is an indication of resistance to blows; flexural strength (right) is an indication of resistance to bending.

distribution along a pole. In general, the closer the balance point is to the grip, the lighter the feel of the pole in use.

Strength is a material's ability to resist breakage or permanent deformation. For ski poles, shaft impact strength and flexural strength are most important. *Impact strength* indicates the lateral impact that a shaft can tolerate without permanent damage. *Flexural strength* is expressed as the lateral force that will buckle or permanently deform the shaft. *Compressive strength* and *tensile strength,* which indicate the maximum compression and tension a shaft will tolerate, are also of interest. These properties are in-

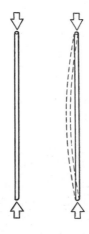

Stiffness indicates how well a shaft stays straight.

volved in the bending characteristics, because bending involves compression on the near side and tension on the far side of the bend. A high tensile-strength material also has a high flexural strength.

Liveliness is a qualitative indication of how much a pole bends when planted in the snow and how quickly it straightens out again when unweighted. The material properties involved are *stiffness,* which indicates the axial force that causes shaft bending, and *elasticity,* which is a measure of how far a shaft bends and springs back again without permanent deformation.

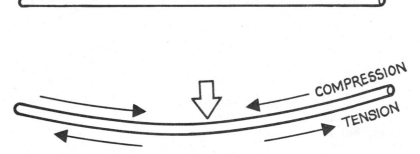

Compressive strength is an indication of shaft sturdiness. Bending causes both compression and tension.

Durability is a qualitative indication of a pole's ability to withstand all destructive forces not due to use in skiing. For instance, durability in a tonkin pole indicates the extent to which pole shafts crack due to drying in storage.

Summing up pole properties, a good pole can be said to have high impact strength, flexural strength, and tensile strength. Its weight should be low and its balance good. Its stiffness should suit its intended use: poles for modern hard-packed racing tracks are stiffer and hence seemingly less lively than those formerly used by racers.

CONSTRUCTION AND MATERIALS

Like skis, the classification of poles is according to the dominant structural material in the shaft. The materials now used are tonkin cane, synthetic fibers, or metal alloys. Pole shafts may be either tapered, with shaft diameter diminishing from grip to basket, or cylindrical, with constant shaft diameter.

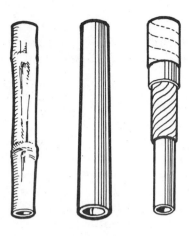

Typical pole shafts, left to right: tonkin, aluminum, synthetic fiber.

Tonkin poles — the traditionals

Tonkin is a natural cane, from a bamboolike grass (*phyllostachys bambusoides*) named for its major source, the coastal regions of southern China around the Gulf of Tonkin. As a pole shaft material, tonkin has good impact strength, good flexural strength, and liveliness.

Prior to export from China, raw tonkin stalks are cut, straightened, trimmed to shipping lengths, sorted, and packed in bales. Cane diameter ranges from 14 to 18 mm ($^9/_{16}$ to $^{13}/_{16}$ in.). In the ski pole factory, tonkin is first inspected and sorted and cut to production lengths. These canes are the "raw material" for tonkin pole shafts, which are then kilned, straightened, lacquered, and paired, ring-against-ring. These pairs are then the finished shafts, ready for pole production.

Tonkin's properties and relatively low cost long made it the dominant shaft material. But the increasing scarcity of quality cane and, in an age of rising labor costs, the many manual operations involved in shaft production have increased the cost of tonkin poles. Also, the processes for and costs of producing the other parts of a pole—the grip, basket, ferrule, and tip—are the same for tonkin poles as for comparable models of poles with synthetic shaft materials. This means that tonkin poles no longer have the low-price advantage that they once enjoyed.

Since tonkin is a natural product, its properties may vary. Also, tonkin shafts may crack as they dry in storage. But tonkin poles are durable and cracks can be repaired at home with tape and glue. As recently as 1978, arctic expedition skiers selected tonkin poles for this very reason: they could easily be repaired by hand if damaged.

Metal poles — alloys give strength

Metal pole shaft tubing is made not of pure metals but rather of alloys, for greater strength and lighter weight.

Poles with both steel alloy and aluminum alloy shafts are available. Aluminum alloy shafts are by far the most common since aluminum is stronger than steel in relation to its weight. (Were this not so, airplanes would be made of steel.)

There are many aluminum alloys, of which about six are suitable for ski pole shafts. Aluminum alloy tensile strength and price both increase with the increased content of expensive alloying metals. Shaft tubing wall thickness and overall shaft diameter and taper depend on the strength of the alloy used. The stronger the alloy, the lesser the amount of metal needed to make a strong pole shaft. The various alloys now used in ski pole shafts are listed in the table.

The 7075 and 7178 alloys, developed for aircraft and space uses, are the strongest (and most expensive) for their weight and thus are used for racing pole shafts. Shafts of 2014 alloy are less expensive, relatively strong, and have good elasticity. Therefore they are used on quality recreational poles. 6061 alloy is used for inexpensive pole shafts. However, its lower strength requires thicker walled shaft tubing and greater shaft diameter, over 16 mm as compared to 15 mm or 16 mm for shafts of 7075, 7178, or 2014 alloys.

ALUMINUM ALLOYS USED IN SKI POLE SHAFTS

Aluminum Association number	Alloying metals	Tensile strength (kp/mm^2)
3004	Mg, Mn	26
6063	Mg, Si	30
6061	Mg, Si	33
2014	Cu, Mg, Si	50
7075	Cu, Mg, Zn	56
7178	Cu, Mg, Zn	63

Cu = Copper, Mg = Magnesium, Mn = Manganese, Si = Silicon, Zn = Zinc
$1 \ kp/mm^2$ = 1420 psi (pounds per square inch)

Synthetic-fiber poles — new and now dominant

Like the structural layers of synthetic-fiber skis, synthetic-fiber pole shaft tubing is made of synthetic fibers bonded in place and given final shape and form by a matrix of hardened resin or plastic material. Shafts are now made with glass, carbon, or a combination of glass and carbon fibers.

Fiberglass shaft tubing consists of structural fiberglass filaments running longitudinally along the tube and/or wound in spirals around the tube, bonded in a polyester or epoxy matrix. Polyester tubing with longitudinal filaments only is the least expensive and the weakest: it has about the same compressive strength as tonkin but has inferior flexural strength and impact strength. When damaged due to impact, such as in a skiing fall, such shafts may shatter or otherwise collapse completely. These disadvantages can be overcome by combining longitudinal and spiral-wound fiberglass in the shaft tube, which is a more costly process. The strongest fiberglass shaft tubing uses longitudinal and spiral-wound fiberglass filaments in three or more layers, bonded in an epoxy matrix. One particularly strong shaft production method involves *cross banding,* which involves winding fiberglass in crossing spirals in both directions around the shaft tube.

Carbon fiber shaft tubing is made by methods similar to those used to produce quality fiberglass shaft tubing. Carbon fiber is more brittle than fiberglass and thus requires more involved production techniques.

Several production methods are currently used, all of which stretch and/or roll the carbon fiber on a tapered mandrel, which is extracted after the epoxy matrix material has cured. Most carbon fiber shaft tubes also contain some fiberglass, usually in the outer surface of the tube, as an armor for the more brittle carbon fiber structural layers. Strictly speaking, these shafts should be designated as fiberglass-armored carbon-fiber shafts, but the term is simply too cumbersome to be useful.

The major advantage of carbon fiber shafts is their extremely light weight, 65 to 85 grams per meter (0.7 to 0.9 ounces per foot) of shaft tubing, compared to 105 to 120 grams per meter (1.1 to 1.3 ounces per foot) for the lightest of aluminum alloy or fiberglass shaft tubing. In addition, carbon fiber shafts may be made stiffer than those of other materials, which is a desirable characteristic for racing poles used on hard-packed tracks. However, as for skis, carbon fiber is an extremely expensive material, and the production processes involved are relatively complex. Therefore, carbon fiber shafts are used only for the most expensive racing poles.

Putting poles together

In general, pole quality is determined primarily by the shaft material used. However, the other pole parts—grip, wrist strap, basket, ferrule, and tip—and the manner in which they are attached to the shaft also affect overall pole quality.

Grips are made of plastic, cork, leather, synthetic leather, or velour (a velvetlike, synthetic fabric resembling suede leather). Plastic grips, which usually are molded in one piece and pressed on the pole shafts, are the least expensive. Cork grips are cemented to shafts along with a retaining mechanism for the wrist strap. Leather and velour grips are actually a covering over a profile formed by the upper end of the pole shaft and an insert, usually of polyethylene plastic. The leather or velour is either glued on the

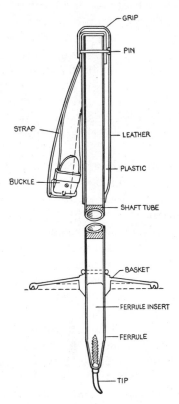

Anatomy of a typical pole.

profile and around the pole or sewn on with nylon thread. Cork, leather, and velour grips are more expensive than plastic grips but are warmer and absorb hand perspiration, which is why they are used on all quality poles.

Wrist straps are usually made of leather, synthetic leather, or nylon webbing. Most wrist straps are adjustable to fit various gloved and bare hand sizes. Strap adjustments may be made either with buckles or with clamp mechanisms built into the top of the pole grip. Low-priced poles often have fixed-length straps.

Baskets are usually made of plastic. The plastic most used is EVA, *ethyl vinyl acetate,* which retains its flexibility and resistance to cracking at low temperatures. Several different EVA compounds are used; the greater the vinyl content, the greater the flexibility in cold weather. Some baskets have outer rings of aluminum alloy or fiberglass-reinforced plastic, attached to the pole with a web of plastic or rubber.

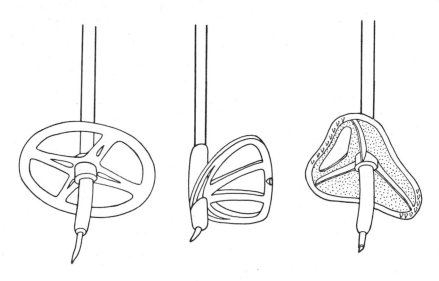

Typical pole baskets, left to right: conventional round, asymmetrical racing, and triangular.

Ferrules, which strengthen the lower end of the pole and provide an anchor for the tip, are made of aluminum alloy or plastic, usually nylon or EVA. The internal part of the ferrule, which anchors the tip inside the shaft, is plastic. The ferrules on some poles, such as racing poles with asymmetrical baskets, are often molded in one piece with the basket and fitted with tips before being mounted on pole shafts.

Tips are made of hardened steel alloy, similar to the type used for the studs on studded snow tires, or of sintered carbide alloys. Tips are either bent forward or cut with a forward-angled taper, the better to grip the snow in poling; midway in the diagonal stride poling movement, the bent or angled part of the tip is vertical to the snow surface. Tips are either pressed or screwed into the anchor inside the ferrule or molded into the ferrule-basket. They usually are mounted and shaped so they may be sharpened after they have become dull in use. Tips of poles for small children are made of plastic for safety.

SO GOES RACING, SO GOES THE SPORT

Most athletes in individual events, like ski racing, are actually conservative in their approach to equipment, preferring to compete equally with their opponents on gear they know to be reliable rather than chancing failure on unproven new gear. But when some racers do well with something new in the way of equipment, all others want it immediately, to enjoy the same advantages it gives. This is why equipment "breakthroughs" are often as much associated with particular ski meets as are the names of the winning racers. In the forefront of ski meets are, of course, the Winter Olympics and FIS World Ski Championships. And an equipment breakthrough has been associated with most of these meets since 1968.

It might have been an American who started it all. In the 1968 Winter Olympics, the Nordic events were held in Autrans, near Grenoble, France. U.S. polemaker Scott was there, equipping some national teams, including the U.S. team and the Russian team, with a new aluminum pole, lighter and stronger than the tonkin racing poles then in use. The Russians took their share of the medals, and presto! everyone wanted aluminum poles. In the 1970 FIS Nordic World Ski Championships in Vysoké Tatry, Czechoslovakia, a few racers showed up in one-piece suits, differing from the two-piece, knicker-blouse suits then in general use. Nobody thought that they were faster clothes, but they looked better, racers thought. Some racers had used a new, molded-sole boot, although most stuck to the still lighter, laminated leather, sewn-sole racing boots then popular, many with white uppers. By the 1972 Winter Olympics in Sapporo, Japan, the picture had changed: almost all racers used Nordic Norm molded-sole boots which fit toe bindings literally full of holes to cut weight. In the 15 km, Norwegian racer Ivar Formo won a bronze medal using a new plastic binding, and plastic bindings were suddenly popular.

In comparing today's cross-country ski equipment picture with that of a few years ago, one man and one race are prominent: Thomas Magnusson of Sweden won the 30-km race, the first event of the 1974 FIS World Ski

POLE TYPES

Poles are classified according to intended use, but in a manner differing from those used for skis, boots, and bindings. There are two main categories: racing and recreational. The recreational category is further broken down into poles for in-track skiing and poles for out-of-track, wilderness, or deep snow skiing. **Racing poles** are designed for use on well-packed tracks only. Shafts are of the strongest aluminum alloys, carbon fiber, or fiberglass, and are usually tapered, with maximum diameters of about 16 mm (⅝ in.) tapering down to about 11 mm (⁷/₁₆ in.). Grips

---

Championships in Falun, Sweden, on fiberglass skis, a first in its own right. Austrian ski makers Kneissl and Fischer had their products on the lion's share of the medalist racers' feet, and the switch from wood to fiberglass was on.

In the 1976 Winter Olympic Nordic events, held in Seefeld, Austria, then-upstart polemaker Exel of Finland touted newer, lighter, stiffer racing poles, with small, asymmetrical baskets and carbon-fiber shafts. Over 70 percent of the medalists used the new Exel poles, and the switch to carbon-fiber poles for racing was on. At the same time, the French division of athletic shoemaker Adidas introduced the Norm 38 boot-binding system, the first where a "snout" on the front of the boot sole fits into a small toe-clip binding. The new boots and bindings were on the feet of the Russians, who, as usual, picked up more than their share of the medals— but the newness didn't guarantee complete success: due to weaknesses caused by inhomogeneous injection of the boot sole, several boots broke at the toe. Russian Evgeniy Beliaev, first out and leading for the USSR in the four-man, 40-km relay, broke a boot and lost almost four minutes borrowing a replacement ski and boot from a spectator, which dropped him to tenth place for the lap. But his teammates ran one of the more spectacular relays to date, and Russia ended up third, with a bronze medal for the event.

By the 1978 FIS World Ski Championships, in Lahti, Finland, all racers used synthetic-fiber skis, carbon-fiber or special aluminum alloy poles, "snout" boots and bindings (Norm 38 or Racing Norm) and one-piece suits, many full-length, down to the ankle. It was, on the equipment picture, a battle of brands, not of technologies.

What's accepted in racing usually comes more gradually to recreational skiing: two to three seasons between racing breakthrough and recreational widespread use seems to be the rule.

So goes racing, so goes the sport.

are of cork, leather, or velour, and wrist straps, made of leather or nylon webbing, are adjustable. Some wrist straps feature an attached small elastic loop, intended to fit over the wrist to hold the strap firmly in place in racing. Baskets, which are angled to shafts, are made in a variety of asymmetrical shapes—triangular, hoof-shaped, forked, etc.—and are usually 7 to 9 cm (2¾ to 3½ in.) in maximum dimension. These "half baskets," which project rear-

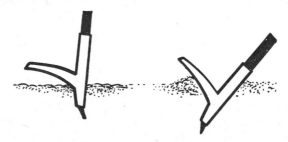

Asymmetrical baskets ease poling on hard-packed racing tracks.

ward, have no front part ahead of the shaft. They are designed for maximum ease of pole plant and withdrawal on packed racing tracks. Pole pair weights (140 cm) are as low as 280 gr (10 oz.). Shafts are stiffer than those of recreational poles for maximum poling efficiency in hard, machine-packed racing ski tracks.

Recreational poles are available with aluminum alloy, fiberglass, or tonkin shafts. Shaft diameters are from 14 to 16 mm (9/16 to 5/8 in.) and may be cylindrical or tapered, except for tonkin shafts, which are cylindrical only. Grips are made of plastic, leather, synthetic leather, velour, or cork, and wrist straps are adjustable or fixed. Poles for skiing on prepared tracks usually have small, round baskets, up to 9.8 cm (3¾ in.) in diameter, or asymmetrical, like the baskets on racing poles. Poles for out-of-track skiing in wilderness and/or deep snow have larger, round baskets, 12 to 14 cm (4¾ to 5½ in.) or more in diameter. Some pole makers offer accessory baskets, about 15.5 cm (6⅛ in.) or more in diameter, designed to fit over pole baskets for better basket ride on top of deep, powder snow. Pair weights (140 cm) are about 400 to 500 gr (14 to 17.7 oz.).

Children's poles resemble recreational out-of-track poles and usually have plastic grips. Shafts are usually about 12 mm (15/32 in.) in diameter, thinner than those for adult-sized poles, and may be of tonkin, aluminum alloy, or fiberglass. Tips on poles for tots are usually of plastic as a safety measure, to avoid injury in falls.

8 CLOTHING

From the standpoint of survival, clothes are more necessary for skiing than skis are: nature has not equipped humans to deal unaided with the cold of the climates involved.

With virtually no body hair, humans are biologically warm-blooded, tropical animals. Body temperature is regulated almost entirely by processes operating through the temperature-regulating center in the hypothalamus, a part of the brain. The function is sort of a body thermostat, set to maintain internal temperature within comfortable and safe limits.

Body temperature regulation involves many processes. It can regulate metabolism, or the rate at which heat is produced in the body. Faced with cold, it can constrict blood flow in the veins of the extremities, reroute blood flow, or initiate shivering, an involuntary muscular activity that steps up heat production. Faced with heat, it can step up blood flow and initiate increased perspiration.

These processes are limited in their ability to cope with extremes. Although some peoples, such as the Australian Aborigines, can sleep naked comfortably, without shivering, at temperatures down to freezing, most humans need insulation to cope with low temperatures. From a purely scientific viewpoint, this may be why most of the world's peoples wear clothes!

For cold conditions, such as those encountered in skiing and other outdoor winter activities, the purpose of clothing is to cut heat loss to the point where the body's temperature regulation processes can keep up with the heat loss. Although a few streakers have been seen on skis, skiers are usually completely clothed with good reason: for most skiable weather conditions, skiing would otherwise be impossible.

TEMPERATURE IS THE KEY

Body temperature is perhaps the most familiar measure of body function, as most persons first experience having their temperature taken in early childhood. The temperature measured for medical purposes is the body core, or internal body temperature, which depends on where it is measured. The average rectal temperature for normal, resting adults is 37°C (98.6°F) and the oral temperature is 36.7°C (98.1°F). Variations of 0.5°C (0.9°F) from these values can be expected in healthy individuals. Exercise can increase body temperature by as much as 2.5°C (4.5°F). This means that the healthy, average human body functions best at an internal core temperature of 36.5° to 39.5°C (97.7° to 103.1°F).

When at rest in temperatures lower than 27°C (80.6°F) in air or 33°C (91.4°F) in water, the human body loses heat to the surrounding environment. At higher temperatures, it absorbs heat from the environment. Temperature regulation, aided by human ingenuity, aims to balance body heat production against body heat loss to maintain optimum internal body core temperature.

Skiing is a cold-weather activity, so the major physiological concern is to conserve body heat to maintain body temperature. Lowered body core temperature, as may be caused by prolonged exposure to cold, degrades physical performance. When body core temperature falls by just 2°C (3.6°F) to 35°C (95°F), oxygen uptake, which fuels motion, drops. Further temperature decrease to subnormal levels may result in *hypothermia* (the opposite of *hyper-*thermia, excessively high body temperature), in which nervous system functions, muscular movement, and circulation are impaired.

Prolonged or excess hypothermia can be lethal. There is no exact lower body temperature that is known to be fatal, but few humans can survive when body core temperatures fall below 25°C (77°F), although several cases are on record of persons surviving body temperatures as low as 16°C (61°F), usually when in a drunken stupor.

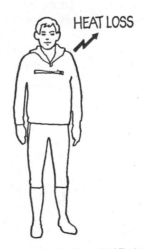

HEAT LOSS

When at rest in air temperatures lower than 81°F, the body loses heat to the environment.

Reduced skin temperature also degrades physical performance. Cooling of the skin usually involves cooling of the underlying muscles. Muscle temperatures below 27°C (81°F) can lead to localized muscular fatigue. In endurance skiing, such as in longer races, there comes a time when the body cannot produce enough heat energy to evaporate perspiration, and local muscle cooling occurs, lowering efficiency and sometimes causing cramps. Hands and feet are particularly vulnerable to lowered skin temperature. At skin temperatures of 10°C (50°F) or below, hand movements are considerably slowed, and nerve function is impaired.

Humans have some physiological adaptability to cold, but their major defense against cold is their ability to avoid it.

BODY HEAT PRODUCTION

Food is the source of energy for the body. Food consumed reacts with oxygen in the metabolic process to liberate energy. For an average adult at rest, the ordinary diet liberates an average of 4.83 kilocalories per liter of oxygen consumed. The kilocalorie is one thousand calories. In describing the energy content of diets, it is usually shortened to Calorie, correctly spelled with a capital C.

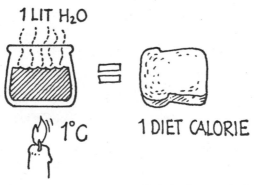

1 LIT H₂O

1°C

1 DIET CALORIE

One kilocalorie (in physics) equals one Calorie (in nutrition).

At sea level and at an average respiration, air breathed in contains 0.25 liters of oxygen per minute, so the average human metabolism then proceeds at a rate of 1.21 Calories per minute, or about 73 Calories per hour. This is the number often quoted as the minimum human existence requirement, a diet supplying 1800 Calories per day.

The energy liberated by the metabolic process is used in many ways. About 5 percent is converted immediately into heat. About

131

45 percent is wasted in the various processes that convert food and oxygen into useful body chemicals. This wasted energy is eventually given off as heat. From 20 percent to 45 percent is used to fuel the body's continuous internal activities such as circulating blood, breathing, and digesting foods. This energy also finally appears as heat. From 0 percent to 25 percent is available for physical activity.

At rest the total average adult metabolic activity corresponds to a power of 1.05 watts per kilogram (2.2 pounds) body weight when sleeping and 1.3 watts per kilogram when awake. This is why a

CAREFUL WITH THE CALORIE!

The calorie is a pretty small unit of energy. As we all recall, or perhaps wish to forget, from high-school science classes, the *calorie* is the heat required to raise the temperature of one gram of pure water 1°C. So the *kilocalorie,* 1000 calories, is the heat required to raise the temperature of one kilogram of pure water 1°C.

The kilocalorie is the unit used to measure the energy content of diets. In common usage, the "kilo" is dropped in discussions of diets. Too bad, as the use of "calorie" leads many people to wonder if it's really that mini-unit they learned about in school. It isn't. It's a thousand times larger. So, to avoid confusion, some writers have used "gram-calorie" to denote the little one (remember the gram!), and "calorie" to denote the big one. Now that's really confusing. Think of the confusion at banks if the same words were used for a buck and a grand.

So careful writers (and the writer of this book has tried to be careful) let the calorie be. They call it "the calorie." And they recognize that "the kilocalorie" is a wee too scientific. So they capitalize "Calorie" when they mean a thousand of them, as in diets. The big C for the big one, the little c for the little one.

Soon, care for the calorie may be passé, as the metric system and its related quantities are adopted worldwide. The metric unit of energy is the *joule.* It's even smaller than the calorie: there are 4.18 joules in a calorie. Dieticians now speak in terms of *kilojoules,* and some food products are now labeled using the unit. This means that diet energy numbers are more than four times as large as when people speak in Calories. That's a disadvantage. But there's also an advantage, which helps in relating the energy content of foods to other forms of energy: a joule is equal to a power of one watt for a period of time of one second. So a kilowatt-hour, what you buy when you pay your electric bill, is 3600 kilojoules. Ovomaltine says that a glass of its product (powder, mixed in milk) provides 780 kilojoules. That's 0.217 kilowatt-hours, a little more than the energy needed to run a couple of 100-watt light bulbs for an hour. At rest, the average adult uses about as much energy as an 85-watt light bulb.

Only a quarter of the body's energy consumption is available for motion.

roomful of sitting people, such as an auditorium, can quickly heat up: at an average body weight of 65 kilograms (143 pounds) each person corresponds to an 85-watt heater.

Exercise increases oxygen consumption and the metabolic rate—and therefore the body heat production—to several times the minimum base level. An average recreational cross-country skier produces 540 Calories per hour (625 watts), or 7.5 times the average base rate. At this rate, the average skier "burns" 1800 Calories, the minimum sedentary daily consumption, in just 3 hours and 20 minutes. Rates for cross-country ski racers are even higher. In an average 30-kilometer race, racers "burn" Calories at a rate of 1200 per hour (1400 watts), and rates for shorter sprints or

Standing, touring, and racing involve increasing energy consumptions.

uphill stretches can be even higher, as much as 2100 Calories per hour (2.5 kilowatts!).

These different heat production rates indicate differing needs for insulation to maintain body warmth in cold weather.

BODY HEAT LOSS

Body heat loss is necessary to maintain body temperature. For instance, a 70 kg (154 lb.) racer running at a rate corresponding to a consumption of 1750 Calories per hour (2000 watts) could theoretically suffer a body temperature rise to 60°C (140°F) if heat were not lost.

Body heat is lost through conduction, convection, evaporation, and radiation. All body surface heat losses depend on skin temperature, area, exposure, and heat supply.

The head is usually the warmest part of the body, because it has the greatest blood supply. Because the face and often other parts of the head are usually exposed when skiing, heat loss through the head is high, often a fifth or more of total body heat loss.

Heat loss from the other parts of the body depends on their general shape. The amount of heat produced or stored in a part of the body is proportional to the volume of the part. The amount of heat lost is proportional to the area of the part.

This is why fingers and toes lose heat more rapidly than other

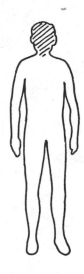

The head is the warmest part of the body.

body parts: they have large surface areas but only small volumes. For the same reason, arms and legs lose heat more rapidly than the torso.

Conduction is the transfer of heat by direct contact. All materials conduct heat. Air is a very poor heat conductor: it insulates. Clothing fibers conduct heat better than air. This is why clothing insulates primarily because of trapped still air in fibers, yarns, knits, and weaves, and not because of the fibers themselves. There is very little difference among the insulating abilities of various fibers. Insulating ability is determined more by yarn and textile construction. Water is an excellent heat conductor, which is why wet clothing loses much of its insulating ability.

Convection accounts for the greater portion of heat transferred to or from the body to the surrounding air. It depends on a temperature difference. If air temperature is above skin temperature, the body gains heat. If air temperature is below skin temperature, the body loses heat.

For any air temperature, the amount of heat gained or lost by convection depends on the amount of air that comes in contact with the skin surface. This is why wind or body movement in still air

---

STAY WARM, BUT NOT TOO

A feeling of comfortable temperature, or of warmth or chill, is often individual. But there are limits to the temperature extremes humans can tolerate without damage. Protected humans can function in environmental temperatures between $-50°$ and $100°C$ ($-58°$ to $212°F$) but can tolerate a variation of only about $4°C$ ($7.2°F$) in their own internal body core temperatures without impairment.

There apparently are no exact limits for extremes that damage, save those set by biology. The temperatures a living cell can tolerate range from about $-1°C$ ($30.2°F$), when ice crystals forming in the cell break it apart, to $45°$ ($113°F$), when heat coagulates proteins in the cell, in a process similar to coagulation in the white of a boiled egg. Humans can tolerate body temperatures in excess of $41°C$ ($105.8°F$) for short periods of time only. This means that humans, like many mammals, live their entire lives with body temperatures only a few degrees below their thermal death points.

This may explain why nature seems to have equipped us with better defense mechanisms and better early warnings of excess heat than of heat deficiency. The history and literature of cold climates and exploits contain many accounts of the sometimes unconscious suffering of cold. But there seem to be virtually no similar accounts of persons being too hot and not knowing it.

cools: air moving by the skin removes more heat than would be lost to still air at the same temperature.

Convection heat losses can be controlled by reducing the amount of skin exposed and by reducing the amount of air circulating in contact with the skin.

Evaporation cools because heat is required to vaporize water. The evaporation of moisture from the skin and respiratory tract accounts for about one-fifth of the body's normal heat losses.

Respiratory moisture loss depends primarily on the amount of air passing in and out of the lungs. At rest, respiratory moisture loss can be an appreciable portion of the total losses due to evaporation, but during exercise it is always small compared to losses due to evaporation from the skin.

At rest, the body perspires, producing about half a liter (about a pint) of moisture per day. During exercise, perspiration increases, sometimes to as much as a liter (slightly more than a quart) an hour. If the skin is wet by perspiration or outside water, a relatively large amount of heat is required for evaporation. This is why wet skin cools—pleasant in the summer, but potentially hazardous in the winter.

Radiation is the process by which energy is emitted, transmitted through space, and then absorbed. It is independent of physical contact or of an intervening medium, such as air. Radiation is the way the sun illuminates and heats the earth.

Radiation heat losses from the body are relatively small. However, radiation heat gain can be large: on a clear day, the body can absorb as much as three times as much heat energy from sunshine as produced by its own metabolism.

INSULATING THE BODY

Keeping warm and comfortable in cold weather involves insulating, or interfering with the processes that cause body heat loss. The body can be insulated by its own tissues, air, and clothing.

Tissues are relatively good conductors of heat. Their value as insulation depends on their blood supply: the lower the blood supply, the better the insulation, and vice versa. When cooled, the body reacts to increase insulation through vasco-constriction, or blood vessel contraction in the extremities, and through some deviation of blood in the vessels of the extremities from surface to deeper veins. Conversely, when warmed, the body reacts by dilating, or opening up these veins to increase blood flow.

Vasco-constriction acts to preserve warmth in the body core but has the disadvantage that it allows cooling of the extremities. The body's insulating defenses against cold are therefore geared to preserve the vital internal organs at the expense of the extremities. The head is the only part of the body excepted, as the brain must be kept well supplied with blood to keep it working. This is another reason for the relatively high heat loss through the head, and the logic behind the old saying, "If you want to keep your feet warm, wear a cap."

Still air is an excellent insulator, but even slight air movements reduce its insulating value considerably. For instance, a 10 mph wind can remove heat so rapidly that it has only one-fifth the insulating ability of still air.

This loss of the insulating effect of the surrounding air as wind increases is called *wind chill*. The wind chill table is a listing of equivalent still-air temperatures for a range of wind speeds from a slight breeze (5 mph) through a strong gale (50 mph).

WIND CHILL TABLE

Temp- erature (°F)	WIND (miles per hour)								Winds above 40 mph have little additional effect
	5	10	15	20	25	30	35	40	
	Equivalent Chill Temperature								
40	35	30	25	20	15	10	10	10	
35	30	20	15	10	10	5	5	0	**LITTLE**
30	25	15	10	5	0	0	−5	−5	**DANGER**
25	20	10	0	0	−5	−10	−10	−15	
20	15	5	−5	−10	−15	−20	−20	−20	
15	10	0	−10	−15	−20	−25	−30	−30	**INCREASING**
10	5	−10	−20	−25	−30	−30	−35	−35	**DANGER**
5	0	−15	−25	−30	−35	−40	−40	−45	(flesh may
0	−5	−20	−30	−35	−45	−50	−50	−55	freeze
−5	−10	−25	−40	−45	−50	−55	−60	−60	within one
−10	−15	−35	−45	−50	−60	−65	−65	−70	minute)
−15	−20	−40	−50	−60	−65	−70	−75	−75	
−20	−25	−45	−60	−65	−75	−80	−80	−85	**GREAT**
−25	−30	−50	−65	−75	−80	−85	−90	−95	**DANGER**
−30	−35	−60	−70	−80	−90	−95	−100	−100	(flesh may
−35	−40	−65	−80	−85	−95	−100	−105	−110	freeze
−40	−45	−70	−85	−95	−105	−110	−115	−115	within
−45	−50	−75	−90	−100	−110	−115	−120	−125	thirty
−50	−55	−80	−100	−110	−120	−125	−130	−130	seconds)
−55	−60	−90	−105	−115	−125	−130	−135	−140	
−60	−70	−95	−110	−120	−135	−140	−145	−150	

The wind chill effect is most pronounced on the parts of the body usually left exposed, such as the face and hands. Wind can, in fact, supercool the face and, worse, the hands because of their large skin area, even though the rest of the body is well insulated by clothing.

Clothing insulates because it contains trapped, still air. The amount of insulation afforded by clothing is proportional to the amount of still, or dead, air trapped in and between its surfaces. Loss of trapped still air in clothing by external wind, internal air movement, or compression of clothing bulk reduces clothing insulation.

Insulating values are measured in *clo,* a unit in which one clo is the insulation provided by typical office clothing that keeps a sedentary person comfortable in an indoor environment of 21°C (70°F) at a relative humidity of under 50 percent with only slight air movement.

Body tissues can provide from 0.15 to 0.8 clo of insulation; still air alone provides from 0.2 to 0.8 clo. Clothing provides the greatest range of insulating values, from 0 to 5 clo. In these terms, 4.7 clo is an extremely high insulating value, corresponding to the thickest fur coats of arctic animals.

CLOTHING BASICS

Clothing should protect the body yet not interfere with its movements. In cross-country skiing, insulation is the most important protective characteristic of clothing. Arms and legs must be free to move in the various skiing strides and maneuvers. Therefore the construction of thermal insulation used in practical cross-country clothing is different for different parts of the body.

COLD AS HELL?

A scientific, non-theological inquiry into why the Hells of many religions are depicted as hot places might conclude that suffering from heat was known to and dreaded by the peoples of warm climates, where most of the world's religions began. The same inquiry might uncover exceptions, one of which certainly would be from the pre-Christian Viking Age.

Living in a cold climate, the Vikings were the world's first skiers. They knew, respected, and sometimes feared cold weather. According to the Edda Saga, one of the major legends of the Viking Age, "The way to Hell is northwards and downwards." The Viking Hell was a cold place, from which one did not return. Were reincarnated Vikings to reappear today, they might view a household deep-freeze as a place where one keeps the Devil locked up.

Insulation — layers are best

Conditions are seldom constant during a winter day: temperatures rise and fall; wind force and direction change; sunshine varies in intensity and direction. Skier activity also varies during the course of a day's skiing. Racers warm up, race, then cool down. Recreational skiers ski at varying speeds, uphill, downhill, and on the flat, and may stop to rest, eat, or enjoy scenery. *Basic clothing sense means suiting clothing to the varying needs for insulation required by changes in weather and activity.*

There are two ways to adapt clothing to varying needs: (1) vary its insulating value, and (2) vary ventilation.

Varying insulation is virtually impossible if only one material, such as fur, is used. It's far simpler to use several thin layers that can be put on or taken off to vary total body insulation.

Multiple layers also insulate better than a single layer of the same total thickness. This is because more dead air is trapped in and between thin layers than in one thick layer. Furthermore, thin layers trap air in small, confined spaces. Air thus trapped insulates better than the same amount of air in larger, less confined spaces,

Layers are best in combating cold.

because confinement prevents air movement, which removes heat by convection.

Finally, multiple layers allow the use of special-purpose garments, each fulfilling a particular clothing need.

Regulating ventilation is a useful way to vary total body insulation. Dressed in furs, Eskimos have a tropical environment next to their bodies. They vary the insulation of their clothing by regulating ventilation. However, aside from being expensive and, in the case of protected species, sometimes restricted, fur garments are impractical in cross-country skiing both because the range of body movements and of body insulation requirements during the course of a day varies over a greater range than can be accommodated by a single fur garment and because such garments are heavy. *Layers give warmth at minimum weight. Each layer adds more dead air, which increases insulation.*

Even the best of layering can lose some of its value if its function of trapping dead air is defeated. This is why inadvertent ventilation, such as gaps between garments, should be avoided. Adjoining garments should overlap—mittens, for instance, should be long enough to overlap parka sleeves. The rule is: *Overlap to prevent gap.*

Fit is important

Ideally, clothing should fit comfortably, without pressing on the body. It should also allow full freedom of movement and not require more work of the body.

But no set of clothing can meet all these ideal requirements completely. The three major departures from the ideal are constraint, friction, and hobbling: *Constraint* involves limiting body movement to less than would be possible without clothing. *Friction* involves energy wasted in forcing one layer of clothing to slide over another. *Hobbling* involves interference of movement at the joints due to clothing bulk.

Stay dry

Because water is a good heat conductor, wet clothing rapidly loses its insulating value. Clothes may be wet from without, from snow or rain, or from within, from absorbed perspiration.

Outer clothing layers should be water repellent to prevent outside water from entering inner layers, but not completely waterproof. Completely waterproof outer garments seal in body moisture, which then condenses and wets inner garments. For skiing in windy conditions, outer garments should also be windproof to prevent wind from penetrating inner layers and removing trapped insulating air.

Match clothing to activity

Many beginning skiers seek and heed advice on the choice of their ski gear but select their apparel with little regard to their actual needs. Aside from those who know nothing of cold and dress too lightly for any outdoor winter activity, most skiers err on the side of starting out too warmly dressed. The scene on the first couple of kilometers of any trail is familiar: Skiers start at the trailhead dressed in enough clothing to keep themselves toasty warm while ice fishing on a wind-swept lake. Half a kilometer or so up the trail they stop, overheated and sweaty, to remove clothing. Another half a kilometer along they stop again and attempt to "do something" about the chill they now feel from their sweat-wet clothing. The pattern for the day is set: they are either too hot or too cold.

Another scene is almost as familiar: In the warming hut, a stylishly clad skier huddles over a cup of coffee, complaining between shivers of the extreme cold—on a day when many others are skiing comfortably.

The best way to avoid such extremes of discomfort is to dress according to *activity* and *weather*. For the same weather conditions, it's obvious that a person standing still, burning 1.2 Calories a minute (85 watts), a person ski touring, burning 9 Calories a minute (625 watts), and a person racing, burning 20 or more Calories a minute (1.4 kilowatts) should not dress alike. The basic approach is similar to that of heating a house in winter: the smaller the furnace, the more insulation is required to keep the living room warm. A racer, literally carrying a 1.4 kilowatt self-heater, needs less insulation than a touring skier (with a 625-watt self-heater) and far less than a spectator at the race (with an 85-watt self-heater). Although there are many levels of activity and a range of personal physiologies, the most convenient categories of clothing needs are keyed to activity. There are many activity scales, reflecting various overall needs. A scale based on U.S. Army data, useful to mountaineers and explorers, divides activity into three categories: *sleeping, light work,* and *heavy work.* For the purposes of comparing and selecting clothing for cross-country skiing situations, a more convenient scale of three would be *standing, touring,* and *racing.*

Standing with only moderate motion, as does a spectator at a ski race, involves a minimum of muscular activity. Clothing for such a low activity level must insulate well to conserve body heat.

Touring is what most recreational cross-country skiers do. It is a vigorous activity, so clothing for touring should insulate to conserve body heat, but not to the same extent as for standing. Touring clothing should be adjustable to allow excess heat and perspiration to escape.

Racing: when warmed up and racing, a racer's chief clothing problem is to retain body heat, yet get rid of excess heat and perspiration.

Clothe body parts correctly

For clothing purposes, the body can be divided into upper trunk, including torso and arms; lower trunk, including hips and legs; head; feet; and hands.

Upper and lower trunk: Three distinct layer functions are involved in clothing the torso. The main function of the *inner* layer is to *keep the skin dry*. There are now two different approaches to the problem: (1) Transport perspiration outwards, away from the skin. Super-Underwear® and string-fish-net underwear function in this manner. (2) Absorb perspiration while presenting a dry surface to the skin. Wool absorbs from 25 percent to 35 percent of its weight in moisture before it feels wet and therefore has long been a favorite underwear material. However, fast-skiing tourers and racers perspire so rapidly that they quickly soak wool to more than 35 percent of its weight. For these skiers, wool may be worn over a transport layer.

The main function of the *middle* layer is to *insulate*. The greater the insulation needed, the more layers should be used. Multilayer garments should be size-graduated to fit over one another. For racing, the middle layers are often eliminated completely, and most recreational touring skiers will be comfortable with one or two middle layers.

The main function of the *outer* layer is to *protect against the environment,* as well as provide the desired style and appearance. Outer garments should be windproof and/or water-repellent, as required, and should be permeable to vapor from the body.

For the *upper torso,* transport and/or wool underwear followed by insulating layers—such as a sweater or wool or heavy cotton shirt—topped by a stretch or poplin blouse and, for wind and wet, a shell parka is the usual order for touring. Racers usually need only underwear and a stretch racing suit but sometimes use a turtleneck for extra insulation. Down parkas, such as used in mountaineering and Alpine skiing, usually are too warm for touring and also constrain movement and hobble joints.

For *abdomen and legs,* transport and/or wool underwear followed by knickers and knee socks is today's usual order of garb. Socks should extend over knees so that knickers will overlap well. Windproof, water-repellent overpants should always be carried for extra protection in extreme conditions.

Head: A cap is a must for almost all winter conditions and, when covered by a parka hood, is adequate for the most severe encountered in average recreational touring. In cold weather, racers, who wear no parkas, often protect exposed ears with earmuffs.

Feet: The feet are the most often neglected part of the body when it comes to good insulation. Here, the multilayer principle also applies. A thin pair of socks under a medium-weight knicker sock will insulate better than a single thick knicker sock. Boots should fit snugly with no pressure points that can compress socks, reducing their insulating ability. In extreme cold, boots can be covered with overboots.

Hands: Gloves or mittens are a must, even in warmer weather, as the hands should be protected against both cold and chafing from pole grips and wrist straps. Heat loss from the fingers is high, because they have large areas compared to their small volumes. For this reason, mittens are warmer than gloves in extreme cold. Wool is a good hand insulator but inadequate alone, as it isn't strong enough to withstand abrasion from pole grip and strap. Overmitts or patches on mitts protect against this type of damage. Racers use unlined or lined gloves, with ventilated backs to allow moisture escape.

FABRICS AND FIBERS

Almost all cross-country ski clothing is made from fabrics woven or knitted from yarn.

Weaving is the oldest known method of forming fabric, having been developed in many primitive cultures. It involves interlacing two or more sets of yarn, placed at right angles to each other, using a loom. The set of longitudinal yarns stretched on the loom is called the *warp.* The crossing, transverse yarn is called the *weft.* The many varieties of weaving differ from one another in the manner the weft and warp interlace. The three fundamental types of weaving are *plain, twill,* and *satin.* Simplest is the plain weave, in which the weft passes over alternate warp yarns. Poplin, as used in ski suits, is made by a variety of plain weaving. Twill weaving has a diagonal design, formed by interlacing weft yarns with two or four warp yarns, moving in steps to the right or left to form the final fabric design. Gabardine and denim are twill weaves. Satin has relatively long, uncrossed threads, in either the warp or the weft; it is seldom, if ever, used for garments for skiing or other outdoor activities.

Compared to weaving, *knitting* is a relatively new art, being first practiced in Europe in the Middle Ages. In knitting, loops of yarn are interlocked, using needles. The many knitting methods and stitches classify as either *weft* or *warp* knitting. Weft knitting, the oldest, and perhaps most familiar because it includes hand knitting, uses one continuous yarn, and the fabric is produced in horizontal courses. Warp knitting, as done by machines, forms vertical chains, or wales, each having a separate yarn or set of yarns. The wales are tied together by zigzagging yarns from needle to needle. Knits may be single, as in most hand knitting, or double, in which two strands of yarn are knitted in two interlocking layers. Most knitted fabrics for ski clothing are double warp knits. Some ski sweaters, socks, caps, and mittens are weft knits.

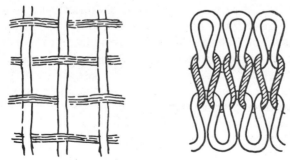

Basic weaving crosses two sets of yarn; basic knitting interlocks one yarn. Shown are simple plain weaving and weft knitting.

Yarn is made by spinning or throwing. Spinning is the conversion of short fibers into continuous yarn. Throwing is the twisting together of continuous filaments, such as silk and manufactured fibers, to produce yarn. Continuous filaments are sometimes chopped into shorter fibers and then spun to produce a bulkier yarn, more closely resembling yarns spun from natural fibers.

Fibers, the "raw materials" for all yarns, are either natural or manufactured. Five characteristics affect use of various fibers in ski apparel.

1. **Strength** involves both tensile strength, or resistance to breaking, and the ability to withstand abrasion.

2. **Insulation,** for dry or wet fibers, indicates how well the final fabrics will insulate.

3. **Resistance** to acids and alkalis indicates how easily a fiber can be dyed and how well it will withstand perspiration, staining, and laundering. Fibers totally resistant to both acids and alkalis cannot be dyed by conventional methods.

4. **Wicking ability** is the ability of a fiber to "pull" and/or transport moisture, like the wick of a candle pulls melted paraffin wax. High wicking ability is desirable for undergarments, to keep the skin dry.

5. **Evaporative ability** describes how well a wet fiber allows moisture to evaporate. High evaporative ability is desirable, to keep clothing dry.

Natural fibers

Natural fibers are of plant, animal, or mineral origin. The overwhelmingly most common in textiles for cross-country ski clothing are cotton, a plant fiber, and wool, an animal fiber. Silk, an animal fiber, is now seldom used in ski apparel.

Cotton fibers are the protective covering of the seeds of the *Gossypium,* or cotton plant. Cotton originated in India, which is where it was found and brought back to Europe in 1350 by the English explorer Sir John Mandeville, who identified it as coming from a "wool plant." Some languages reflect cotton's history: the word for cotton in German is *Baumwolle,* meaning "tree wool." Cotton fiber is about 99 percent cellulose, which is resistant to alkalis but can be attacked by acids. Cotton fiber is stronger when wet than when dry, which is why cotton garments stand up well under repeated launderings. Cotton yarns or fabric are often *mercerized* (after English inventor John Mercer, 1850), or treated with caustic alkali under tension, to increase strength and affinity for dyes. Cotton fibers have a high wicking ability and can retain about 25 times their own dry weight in moisture. This is why cotton is an excellent fiber for towels. But cotton is a poor insulator when wet, which is why high cotton content (50 percent or more) fabrics are avoided in ski apparel.

Wool, unless otherwise specified, comes from the fleece of sheep. Wool from the fleece of other animals is usually so designated: *angora* from the fleece of Angora rabbits or goats, *alpaca* from the South American llama, and so forth.

Wool has relatively good resistance to acids but is easily attacked by alkalis. Wool fibers are extremely resilient and elastic. The natural crimp of wool fibers gives wool yarn bulk, which enables it to trap air and insulate well. Wool can absorb a high amount of moisture, more than other fibers, without feeling damp, which, along with its high volume of trapped air, explains its long use in warm garments.

Two types of fabric are made from wool: woolens and worsteds. The difference is in the yarn. Worsted yarns go through more processes than woolen yarns. Their fibers are arranged parallel to each other and the yarn is even and uniform in diameter. The fibers in woolen yarns are in a conglomerate mass, which gives the final fabrics greater bulk. In ski apparel, worsteds are used in woven materials and in thin sweaters, underwear, and some socks, woolens in sweaters, socks, gloves, mittens, and caps.

Worsted yarn (left) is more regular than woolen yarn (right).

Silk is a translucent, yellowish fiber coated with sericin (a protein), produced by the silkworm in making its cocoon. There are many types of silk-spinning worms, of which the most common is the *Bombyx mori,* or mulberry silkworm. *Sericulture,* the art of cultivating the silkworm, and the weaving of silk fiber into cloth were first practiced in China, according to legend, in 2640 B.C. Each silkworm cocoon yields approximately 750 meters (2,500 feet) of filament. Four to 18 filaments are twisted together to make the raw silk thread, which is subsequently treated and combined with other threads before being woven into cloth. Once used for a wide variety of fine fabrics, silk has virtually been replaced by synthetic fibers for most garments, including utilitarian apparel such as ski clothing.

Manufactured fibers

Manufactured fibers are produced by processes emulating the way the silkworm makes the filament for its cocoon.

In 1889, at the Paris Exposition, Count Hilaire de Chardonnet displayed the first such fabric, made of filaments produced from an extract of mulberry leaves. Chardonnet's "artificial silk," dubbed "rayon" in 1924, was also the first commercially successful artificial fiber and thus the forerunner of today's fiber manufacturing industry.

All manufactured fibers are polymers. That is, they are made up of giant molecules built up from chains of simpler molecules in a process called polymerization. In the final fibers, these giant molecules are aligned parallel to each other, which gives these fibers great strength.

Such fibers are classified as either regenerated or synthetic. *Regenerated* fibers are made from chemically treated natural materials, such as cellulose and protein, and chemically the final fiber is the same material. *Synthetic* fibers are derived from cellulose, coal, or petroleum, through chemical processes, and the final fibers differ chemically from the materials from which they were derived.

Rayon, the first manufactured fiber, may classify either as regenerated or synthetic, depending on the process used for its production. Otherwise, all manufactured fibers now used in ski apparel are synthetics: polyamide, polyacrylonitrile, polyester, polyurethane or polypropylene.

Rayon: Chardonnet's original process for producing the regenerated fiber, involving treating cellulose with nitric and sulfuric acids, is no longer used. Most common now is the *viscose* process, developed in 1892, in which cellulose is treated with carbon disulfide, dissolved in caustic soda, and then hardened with sulfuric acid after being drawn into fibers.

Viscose rayon is used in most wearing apparel, furniture fabrics, and carpets and is marketed under a variety of trade names, such as *Supralan, Swelan, Elaston,* and *Vistra.* More recent is *Model,* a viscose rayon modified by a process similar to mercerizing for greater strength and resistance to curling, used for wash-and-wear fabrics. *Acetate* rayon, or synthetic rayon, is produced by processes first used in England in 1918: cellulose is steeped in acetic acid and then treated with acetic anhydride to form a derived fiber, resistant to stains and creasing. Acetate rayons are marketed under trade names such as *Aceta, Celanese, Fibriceta,* and *Rhodia.*

Triacetate rayons, made by a related process, are marketed under trade names such as *Arnel, Courpleta, Rhonel, Starnel,* and *Tricel.* Rayons are now used in ski apparel mostly in blends with natural fibers, such as with wool in socks, to add strength.

Polyamide fibers are durable and resistant to alkalis but not to acids. They can easily be made into elastic yarns, which is why they are used in fabrics for stretch garments. *Nylon,* the first trade name for polyamide fibers, has now become a generic name for all polyamide materials. It is available in two general types, *nylon 66,* made according to a process developed in the United States, and *nylon 6,* made according to a process developed in Germany. Polyamide, or nylon, fiber materials are marketed under a spectrum of trade names, of which the more common are *Banlon, Bri-Nylon, Nylon, Perlon, Prix-Perlon, Spinlon, Taslan,* and *Ultron.*

Polyacrylonitrile fibers, usually shortened to "acrylic" fibers, have a strength similar to that of cotton and are the lightest fibers now used in ski apparel. They can be spun to resemble wool and therefore are often used in knitted fabrics. They transport moisture well, which suits them to underwear fabrics. They are not as durable as polyamide or polyester fibers, but about twice as durable as wool. They are marketed under trade names such as *Acrilan, Courtelle, Dralon,* and *Orlon.*

Polyester fibers are durable and withstand acid and bleach better than polyamide, but are weaker in alkali resistance. Polyester fibers are moderate insulators and have a low wicking ability and a high evaporative ability. Their major attribute is resistance to curling, which is why they are combined with wool in permanent-press garments. The more common trade names for polyester fiber fabrics are *Dacron, Kodel, Terylene, Tetoron, Trevira,* and *Vestan.*

Polyurethane fibers have high strength and elasticity and are most often used in stretch fibers, marketed under trade names such as *Lycra, Spanzelle, Vyrene,* and *Spandex.*

Polypropylene fibers are good insulators and have high wicking and evaporative abilities. They are resistant to both acids and alkalis. These properties well suit polypropylene to be used in knitted transport-type underwear. The most common trade name for polypropylene fibers is *Montefibre.*

Polyvinyl chloride (PVC) fibers absorb little moisture and resist acids and alkalis. They have good wicking ability and good evaporative ability, and therefore are used in knitted fabrics for underwear. They shrink when washed in hot water, so PVC fiber fabrics must be washed in lukewarm or cold water. PVC fiber textiles are marketed under trade names such as *Rhovyl*.

Manufactured fibers are thrown, or twisted, to make hard-surface yarns, spun to make bulky yarns, or combined in a variety of ways to make textured yarns.

The most common textured fibers in ski clothing are made by processes similar to that used to make *Helanca*. In the Helanca process, continuous, parallel, zig-zag nylon fibers are thrown or spun into elastic yarn. European-made fabrics *Helanca, Spinlon,* and *Ultron* are produced in this manner. Ultron has a wax additive said to make the finished fabric anti-static. *Helanca, Spinlon,* and *Ultron* are used in stretch fabrics for blouses, knickers, sweaters, and ski suits. *Lycra* is made by spinning thin polyurethane fibers around a core of thicker fibers. Thin *Lycra* threads are combined with other fibers to add stretch in socks and caps.

Blends, combinations, and laminates

In cross-country ski clothing, synthetic fibers are used either alone or in various blends or combinations with cotton or wool. The major technical reason for blending fibers is to obtain characteristics not possible with natural or synthetic fibers alone, such as stretch, resistance to abrasion, water repellency, etc. In some fabrics, synthetic and natural fibers are used separately to fully exploit the properties of each: stretch material with polyamid outside and cotton inside for absorbency is a typical example.

Fabrics may also be laminated, or coated with films to achieve specific properties. Rubberized nylon fabrics, as used for wet-weather garments for sailing and similar activities, are examples of coated fabrics. An example of the laminates is *Gore-Tex,* a trade name for a microporous laminate that is breathable yet highly water repellent. Gore-Tex is usually laminated onto lightweight, strong fabrics for use in garments designed to be water repellent.

Laundering and cleaning

Correct laundering or cleaning of garments depends on the fabrics, dyes, weaves, or knits, and on the treatments used. For synthetic fibers, the fiber chemical family is decisive.

As a general rule, colored synthetics should not be washed with white garments, as their dyes can run. Most ski garments are now labeled with international symbols indicating the correct washing or cleaning method to be used.

Laundering is indicated by the outline of a washtub with the maximum wash water temperature:

cold wash	30°C = 86°F
fine wash	40°C = 104°F
warm wash	60°C = 140°F
hot wash	95°C = 203°F

Fabrics that should not be laundered are indicated by a cross through the tub symbol.

LAUNDERING	95° BOIL 95°C	60° WARM 60°C	40° FINE 40°C	30° COLD	DON'T WASH
BLEACHING	BLEACH				DON'T BLEACH
IRONING	HIGH 210°C	MED. 160°C		LOW	DON'T IRON
DRY CLEANING	(A) ALL	(P) NORMAL		(F) MILD	DON'T CLEAN

Laundering and cleaning symbols.

Ironing is indicated by the outline of an iron, with either a maximum iron temperature (usually in °C) or one, two, or three dots for low, medium, or high iron temperature:

•	low	120°C = 248°F
••	medium	150°C = 302°F
•••	high	210°C = 410°F

The iron symbol usually is crossed out for no-iron, wash-and-wear fabrics.

Bleach is indicated by a triangle. The letters "Cl" in the triangle indicate that the fabric tolerates chlorine bleach. If the triangle is crossed out or absent, the fabric should not be bleached.

Dry Cleaning is indicated by a circle, with letters inside the circle indicating:

A: All dry cleaning methods
P: Normal methods, as used by cleaners
F: Mild cleaning methods only

The circle is crossed out for fabrics that do not tolerate dry cleaning.

In addition to classification by their constituent yarns, fabrics are classified according to weight and type of weave or knit.

Fabric weight — specifications vary

Four methods are now in use to specify the weight of fabrics:
Weight per unit length, usually ounces per yard. Used mostly for woolens and worsteds. U.S. specification is weight in ounces for a 36-inch length of 56-inch-wide material; British specification is for 37 inches of 58-inch-wide material. The system is used mostly for specification of the more expensive fabrics for men's suits.

Weight for a given length of yarn used in a fabric is sometimes used when fabric fineness is expressed. Most common is the *denier,* a unit of weight for silk and regenerated and synthetic fiber filaments and yarns. The denier number of a fabric is the weight in grams for 9,000 meters (9,840 yards) of the filaments or yarn of which it is composed. The denier is most often used to indicate the fineness of women's hosiery.

Length per unit weight, usually yards per pound. Used mostly for poplins and duck.

Weight per unit area. This is the most modern measurement system, now used internationally. In the United States, it is stated in ounces per square yard of fabric. European fabrics are designated in grams per square meter. To convert grams per square meter into ounces per square yard, divide by 34. The system is now so common that the unit of area is often dropped in catalog data: "2 oz. nylon," for example, means 2 ounces per square yard. Windproof poplins range from slightly less than 100 gr (about 3 oz.) to about 150 gr (4½ oz.), and the crepe stretch materials now used in cross-country clothing from 250 gr (7.3 oz.) to 500 gr (15 oz.).

Fabric types

The fabrics most commonly used in cross-country ski clothing are, alphabetically:

Corduroy: A ribbed fabric, usually of cotton or cotton-synthetic, usually heavy. Higher qualities are hard-wearing and abrasion resistant and therefore are much used in knickers for ski mountaineering. Corduroy's appearance also suits it to use in other cross-country ski fashions.

Crepe: (1) Lightweight synthetic or synthetic-cotton fabric, crinkling surface, usually stretch, used in ultralight garments, such as wind suits. (2) Texturized synthetic, usually nylon fibers crimped and curled by heat; makes filament yarn bulkier and more elastic. Often used in knitted cross-country suits and socks.

Duck: Close-woven, heavy fabric, usually of cotton or cotton-synthetic. Originally used for military uniforms and tents. Used for cross-country clothing accessories such as mittens and gaiters because of its durability and abrasion resistance.

Knitwear or knitgoods: common fabric for cross-country ski clothing. Usually synthetic or synthetic-cotton. Characterized by slight ribbed surface. Usually, but not always, made in two-way stretch. Can be two-sided, such as nylon outside and cotton inside.

Oxford cloth: Twill-weave textured fabric, usually of cotton-synthetic, used for parkas.

Pile fabric: With a nap that resembles fur. Used in jacket, knicker, warm-up suit, mitten, and boot linings. Usually of synthetic or synthetic-cotton blend.

Poplin: From the French "popeline," a smooth-surfaced cloth of cotton or a blend of cotton and synthetic. The most common blend in ski clothing is "60/40," a fabric comprising 60 percent synthetic (polyamide or polyester) and 40 percent tight-twisted cotton. Synthetic poplins, usually 100 percent polyamide, are also available under various trade names. Poplins are usually windproof and usually are treated, coated, or laminated for water repellency. Poplins are used in parkas, knickers, ski suits, wind- and waterproof oversuits, and accessories such as mitten shells and gaiters.

Rib knit: Knit with lengthwise ribs, more elastic than plain knit. Usually in wool or wool-synthetic. Used in sweaters, socks, and caps.

Terry cloth: Cotton or synthetic fabric with uncut loops forming a pile. Traps air and insulates well. Used for absorbent lining in jackets, knickers, and warmup suits.

Taffeta: Fine, plain-weave fabric, usually extremely lightweight, usually synthetic. Used in windproof garments.

Velour: From the Latin "villosus," meaning "hairy." Napped, thick cloth, usually synthetic, used in some linings.

Garment utility depends on fabric characteristics

Fabric characteristics such as thermal insulating value, water repellency, water-vapor resistance, and air permeability determine final garment characteristics.

Thermal insulation of fabrics is measured in *clo*. For a temperature difference of one degree Celsius (1.8°F), 1 clo of insulation allows 5.5 Calories of heat to escape per hour through each square meter of area. Another unit, the *tog*, is also used: 1 clo = 1.55 tog.

Water vapor resistance indicates how well fabrics will allow body moisture to escape. It is measured as the thickness of a layer of still air that would have the same resistance as the fabric in question.

Air permeability is a measure of windproof characteristics. It is measured in terms of the volume of air in milliliters passing through an area of one square centimeter of the fabric at a wind-produced pressure difference of 1 centimeter of water manometer pressure (about one millibar).

Water repellency: Unlike the repellency specifications for leathers, there are no fixed definitions of repellency for fabrics. In general, waterproofing specification involves a test in which the fabric is sprayed with one liter of water per minute from a height of four feet for 24 hours. Classification as "waterproof" demands that this test not alter the chemical or physical properties of the fabric, including air permeability. In general, "water repellent" implies treatment with silicones and/or other chemical compounds. These treatments wear and need periodic renewal.

Clothing performance parameters are seldom stated in numbers. At best, utility is indicated by specification of fabric type and location in the finished garments. This apparently universal lack of concise specification for clothing has the obvious disadvantage that it makes comparison of similar garments more difficult, more subjective than might otherwise be the case.

But one advantage may lie in the sheer difficulty of specifying clothing for persons whose physiology, activity, adaptation to cold, and concept of comfortable temperature vary widely. No matter how accurately a numbered performance system might be devised, it's doubtful that mothers ever would admonish their children to "add half a clo of clothing" instead of "put on another sweater"— although when building a new home, families may well request an additional few inches of insulation to cut energy loss and reduce fuel bills. That clothing is still not specified in numbers when sold is but one of the many confirmations that humans are still more complex than the houses in which they dwell.

Nonetheless, measured clothing performance, expressed in numbers, is extremely useful in clothing research, evaluation, and testing. Here measurement is almost always used to back up subjective testing, in a continuous effort to put numbers on the age-old question, How cold is cold?

A recent series of tests on cross-country ski clothing is shown in the "performance parameters" table. The data tabulated confirms practical experience. Wool knit gloves, caps, and socks are warm but let air through easily. Shell parkas, though themselves poor insulators, usually are windproof. The obvious optimum clothing for warmth and wind protection then comprises multiple layers of tricots or other knits covered by a shell parka for wind protection.

PERFORMANCE PARAMETERS OF TYPICAL RECREATIONAL CROSS-COUNTRY SKIING GARMENTS

			Parameters Measured		
Garment	Fabric, fiber	Fabric weight in oz. per sq. yd.	Thermal resistance in clo	Water vapor resistance cm air equiv.	Air perm-eability ml/cm per sec.
Cap	knitted wool	18	0.63	0.84	81.85
Undershirt	cotton string	8	0.15	0.27	149.91
Shirt	cotton flannel	4	0.10	0.28	69.82
Parka A	polyester/cotton poplin	4.5	0.06	0.22	4.14
Parka B	nylon tricot	7	0.07	0.15	6.71
Mittens	nylon poplin, lined with nylon fleece	3.5 15	1.56	1.51	1.18
Gloves	knitted wool	18	0.94	0.92	145.17
Long johns	knitted cotton	8	0.16	0.28	7.50
Knickers A	polyester/cotton, cotton lining	4.5 4	0.06 0.07	0.46	4.14 9.86
Knickers B	nylon tricot, 2 layers	14	0.26	0.30	6.71
Kneesocks	wool knit	18	0.37	0.53	125.64

Adapted from: Z. Vokac, V. Köpke, and P. Keül, Textile Research Journal, Vol. 42, No. 2 (February 1972), Table III, p. 127.

The performance of this common clothing combination varies, of course, with the type, quality, and number of inner and middle insulating layers and the characteristics of the outer shell parka.

DRESS LIGHT IS RIGHT

The most common clothing error made by neophyte cross-country skiers is to dress too heavily and too warmly. This is because many initially believe that skiing requires as much clothing as more sedentary activities, such as snowmobiling. But the active nature of cross-country skiing dictates the clothing maxim:

dress light is right. *All variable clothing needs–varying needs for insulation and/or water/windproofness–can be accommodated by varying the number of light layers used.*

Start from the skin: Dressing for cross-country starts with the inner underwear layer, whose main function is to keep the skin dry while providing insulation. Avoid cotton underwear as cotton absorbs and holds moisture, making cotton cloth garments wet and clammy. Racers and light-touring skiers should choose moisture-transport type underwear; less active recreational skiers may use wool or wool-synthetic blends. Skiers whose skins are irritated by wool should wear thin transport-type underwear under wool garments.

Then add insulation: What goes over underwear depends on skier activity and weather. Recreational skiers should wear a shirt or sweater. Select sweaters or shirts that are cut long. Standard cuts are usually so short that they will ride up, exposing part of the back when worn under a two-piece suit.

Outer layer important: The outer clothing layer covers slightly more than two-thirds of the body and therefore is not only the most important garment but also the most visible part of skier attire. Garment type and material depend on skiing conditions and personal preference.

Many cross-country skiers—especially wilderness skiers and snow campers—opt for *utilitarian clothing,* such as the durable wool knicker and poplin parka combination long the standby for mountaineers. These garments generally withstand hard use far better than specialized ski apparel and may also be used for other outdoor activities.

Ski apparel can be defined as clothing specifically designed for skiing. The most popular ski garments among recreational cross-country skiers are now two-piece, knicker-jacket suits. These suits are available in several fabrics, of which *nylon knits* are perhaps the most common. Fabric weights vary from 7 to 15 ounces per square yard. *Nylon-cotton knits,* with 60 percent to 80 percent nylon outside and 40 percent to 20 percent cotton inside, are designed for greater insulation and moisture absorption. The inner cotton is sometimes knit in terry, which traps air for better insulation. *Poplin-knit* combinations are made in a variety of ways. Some suits have poplin fronts for wind protection and knit backs for stretch. Others are mostly poplin with stretch panels of knit fabric. *Lined suits* and multilayer suits are designed for greater warmth and/or water and wind repellency.

Though most ski suits feature the traditional to-the-waist knickers, bib knickers have become more popular the past two seasons. Aside from style, one advantage of the bib design is that the back is all covered and therefore less easily exposed should undergarments or turtleneck ride up.

One-piece suits are now standard for racers and are gaining in popularity among light-touring skiers. Lightweight and close-fitting, they allow maximum freedom of movement. The materials used are the same as those used in recreational two-piece suits. There are two types of closure, or suit entry: full-suit front zipper, and shoulder zipper. Shoulder zipper suits can be made more windproof than the front zipper variety but are slightly more difficult to put on or take off. There are two basic suit types: to-the-knees knicker type and to-the-ankle full-length type. The knicker suit uses the traditional kneesocks; the full-length suit is said to eliminate the construction at the knee otherwise necessary to hold socks up and knickers down. Both types are currently used in racing. Full-length suits are difficult to fit, as no one set of sizes and cuts can adjust to the different combinations of torso and leg lengths. Therefore, full-length suits probably will not be marketed in quantity for recreational skiers. All one-piece suits have the drawback that they make calls of nature difficult or uncomfortable to answer when one is away from the conveniences of indoor plumbing.

Kneesocks are available in wool, synthetics, and blends. Wool socks insulate well but tend to collect snow more easily than synthetic socks. Some socks use acrylic legs for water repellency and wool-synthetic stretch feet for warmth and fit. Socks should be chosen long enough to come up above the bottom of the knickers so as not to leave a gap at the knee. Stretch kneesocks should be rolled, not pulled on. This is because pulling stretches the sock too thin over the foot and heel, which accelerates wear.

Gaiters are cloth coverings for the ankles that extend down over boots to seal out snow and are essential for out-of-track skiing in deep snow. There are two general types: ankle gaiters and knee-length gaiters. Ankle gaiters usually are made in one piece, with an elastic seal around the ankle and a strap that runs under the boot or a hook that fixes to the boot laces. Knee-length gaiters are usually made with lace, Velcro, or zipper closures their entire length to allow their being put on or taken off without removing boots. They fix to boots using the same mechanisms as used for ankle gaiters. In addition to increasing water repellency, gaiters add insulation and thus, for the legs, can form the third, outer layer.

Hands—warmth and wear important: Mittens are superior to gloves in insulating the hands. Here, for most recreational skiing, the layer principle is best: wool liners inside poplin mitts allow maximum variation of insulation. Wool mitts should not be worn alone, as they wear quickly from pole strap abrasion. For cold conditions pile-lined poplin mitts can be used alone or over a thin wool mitt. Racers usually prefer gloves, which allow maximum hand freedom in poling. Racing gloves should have ventilated backs to allow hand moisture to escape.

Caps—knits best: Knit caps are warm enough for all but the most extreme polar conditions. Wool, wool-synthetic blends, and pure synthetics are used. Wool is warmest, while the synthetics hold their shape best. Knit caps have poor wind resistance but are excellent head insulation when covered by a parka hood.

SIZE CONVERSIONS

Many items of European-made clothing sold in the United States and Canada are labeled with European sizes only. Approximate conversions to U.S. sizes follow.

Suits and Parkas

Men's Sizes

	U.S.	European
Small	36	46
Small	38	48
Medium	40	50
Large	42	52
Large	44	54
Extra Large	46	56
Extra Large	48	58

Women's Sizes

U.S. Women's	U.S. Misses	European
		38
	8	40
34	10	42
36	12	44
38	14	46
40	16	48
42	18	50
44	20	52

Underwear

If stated in numerical sizes, European underwear uses the same designations as ski suits. The more common size ranges follow:

European	U.S.	
	Men's	Women's
Small	36-38	34
Medium	40	36-38
Large	42-44	40-42
Extra Large	46	44-46

Gloves and mittens

European sizes are the same as U.S. sizes, children's and adult's 7 through 10.

Socks

European-made socks use the same sizing as U.S. full sizes, 4 through 13. Approximate sock sizes corresponding to shoe sizes are given in the table:

European	Shoe size			Sock size
	Approximate U.S.			
	Children's	Men's	Women's	
22-23	6-6½			4
24-25	7-8			5
26-27	8½-9½			6
28-30	10-12			7
31-33	13	1	1½-3	8
34-37		2-4	4-6	9
38-40		5-7	7-9	10
41-43		8-9	10-11	11
44-45		10-10½	12	12
46-		11-	13	13

9 WAXES

The gliding of skis and sled runners on different snows is an extremely difficult subject.
—Fridtjof Nansen, 1930

It's been almost 50 years since polar explorer Nansen wrote that introduction to an article describing his long experience with sleds and skis on snow. Today's waxes and waxing methods eliminate most of the problems of Nansen's time, but the principles remain the same—snow has not changed.

THE WHY

A correctly waxed cross-country ski both grips and glides. This is because the microscopic irregularities in the snow surface dig into the wax just enough to allow a motionless ski to grip. But when the ski is in motion, the snow irregularities cannot bite into the wax. They may, in fact, even melt imperceptibly to let the ski glide on a

---

SIERRA LIGHTNING

The first successful cross-country ski wax was a klister, developed in 1913-14 by Peter Östbye. Up until that time, attaining both grip and glide for wetter snow conditions was difficult. At very low temperatures, a smooth wood base would both grip and glide, but as temperatures approached or went above freezing, snow moisture content degraded both glide and grip.

Glide was the lesser problem. Several glide preparations were used, ranging from paraffin candle wax to *Sierra Lightning,* a downhill racing concoction brewed by the California miners in the 1860s. Its ingredients: 2 oz sperm oil, ¼ oz pine pitch, ⅛ oz camphor, 1 tablespoon balsam fir, 1 tablespoon oil of spruce.

Grip was attained by an amazing array of devices, the oldest of which was the fur-based "kicker" ski dating from Viking times. In the late nineteenth century, various fur strips and serrated wood and metal bases were also developed.

But klister and other cross-country ski waxes subsequently developed resulted in superior ski performance that made the earlier bases obsolete. For years, the pre-wax-era ski bases were to be seen only in ski museums.

The recreational cross-country skiing renaissance of the 1960s brought new skiers to the sport, many of whom were little inclined to learn traditional ski waxing. To meet the needs of these skiers, the pre-wax-era ski bases were resurrected in modernized versions as "waxless" skis.

microscopic water layer. The better the waxing job, the greater the difference between grip and glide. The ultimate goal in waxing is for a ski with the best glide to have the best grip also. Technically, waxing increases the difference between static (standstill) and dynamic (in motion) coefficients of friction.

Departing from this ideal, a ski may be waxed incorrectly in two ways: "too hard," and "too soft." If the wax applied is too hard for the snow involved, the snow particles cannot bite into the wax, even when the ski is motionless and weighted. The ski only slips; it won't grip. If the wax is too soft for the snow involved, the snow particles bite into the wax continuously, even when the ski is in motion. The ski then only grips; it won't glide. It may then even allow the snow particles to penetrate far into the wax, which causes the wax to collect snow and ice up.

The secret of waxing is to judge the snow correctly and then select and apply the correct wax.

THE WAXES

Ski wax describes not just one or two products, but a range of products intended for application on the bases of skis. The types of wax products now available fall into general categories of *preparation, base waxes, final waxes,* and *cleaners.*

Preparation: There are two types of base preparation: *impregnation* for wood ski bases and *paraffin waxes* for plastic ski bases.

Impregnation for wood ski bases has two purposes: to protect the skis and to aid wax adhesion. Wood ski bases must periodically be

---

DUBIOUS LORE SOMETIMES DIES HARD

As late as 1970, at least one ostensibly authoritative book on cross-country skiing advised readers to bury their skis in snow in the autumn to allow them to soak up moisture before being used.

The custom has some utility, for *solid wood* skis, such as those made until the mid 1930s. In hot summer storage, solid wood skis often dried out and became brittle: a little absorbed moisture sometimes prevented their breaking when first used on snow of a winter.

However, absorbed moisture damages laminated skis, both by degrading the camber, or letting the skis "go soft," and by providing water that can freeze into ice when the skis are put on snow.

The best treatment for wood skis is to clean and prepare their bases at the end of a season, and store them in a cool, relatively dry place. Moisture is their enemy. Burying laminated skis in snow is a dubious practice that does little more than shorten ski life.

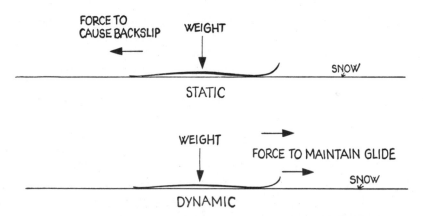

FORCE TO
CAUSE BACKSLIP   WEIGHT

STATIC

WEIGHT

FORCE TO MAINTAIN GLIDE
SNOW

DYNAMIC

Static coefficient of friction determines grip and should be as high as possible. Dynamic coefficient of friction determines glide and should be as low as possible.

impregnated to seal out water and moisture. Wood absorbs water easily, and at low temperatures, absorbed water will freeze. Wax will not adhere to water or ice, and ice expands, which ruins wood bases. There are two main types of impregnating compounds: air-dry base preparation, which is either sprayed on or brushed on, and warm-in tars, which require heat in application. Bases should be prepared whenever the base wood turns white. For most recreational skiers, once at the end of each season is adequate.

Paraffin waxes for preparing plastic ski bases both protect the base and increase glide. They are usually applied on the tip and tail thirds of the base and warmed in for good bond to the base plastic.

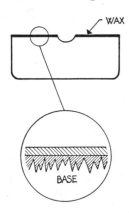

WAX

BASE

Wax binds well to base preparation.

Base waxes are durable binders used as a first layer for snows that abrade wax and skis, such as icy tracks. There are two types: *hard base waxes,* which may be used under all final waxes, and *base klisters,* for use under klister. Base klisters are sometimes called hard-ice klister.

Final waxes are those that contact the snow for the desired waxed performance. There are four types: *Hard wax* is used on dry snow. *Klister-wax* is used on snow at freezing temperatures or on "moist" new snow. *Klister* is a tacky fluid, used on wet snow, coarse dry snow, and icy tracks. *Glide wax* is used to increase glide on skis with various plastic bases, such as polyethylene.

Cleaners are fluid solvents that are brushed or sprayed on ski bases to remove old wax.

Defining your needs — three categories

All waxing procedures involve two or more of the following steps:
- Cleaning—frequent, and always before skis are to be stored.
- Base preparation—for some, but not all bases. Frequency depends on use.
- Base waxing—usually used only by expert recreational skiers and racers.
- Final waxing—always. Method depends on skier experience and preference. *Wide-range* recreational waxing involves using only two waxes. Waxing ease is attained at a slight sacrifice in waxed ski performance for some snows. *Full-range* waxing involves selecting among and using up to ten or more waxes to match more exactly all possible snow conditions. In general, beginners and many recreational skiers may prefer the ease of wide-range waxing, but more skilled recreational skiers and racers are likely to seek the performance available in using a full range of waxes.

The extent to which you should become involved in these various waxing procedures, or how much wax and waxing gear you should have, depends on your needs as a skier. The best waxing is that which best suits your needs. If you are in doubt, start analyzing your waxing needs by defining your skiing. Do you:

1. Ski for recreation and enjoyment?
2. Ski avidly, frequently, and far?
3. Seek maximum skiing speed, as in racing?

If you ski for *recreation and enjoyment,* it's best to keep waxing simple and convenient. For almost all snows, you'll need only two wide-range waxes, types specially suited for broad ranges of snow conditions, usually one for temperatures below freezing and one for temperatures above. Beginners should always start with wide-range waxing.

If you are an *avid cross-country skier,* you probably are willing to spend more time waxing to attain the performance better waxing affords. Your needs are best fulfilled by a selection of waxes, usually about five, with the types depending on the snow conditions and temperatures where you most often ski.

If you seek *speed,* as in racing or citizens' racing, you'll want to "fine tune" your skis for best performance on all snows. This requires learning the properties of and using a full line of as many as 19 waxes, base waxes, and preparation compounds. This advanced form of waxing takes time and requires skill, but it pays off in the ultimate of ski performance.

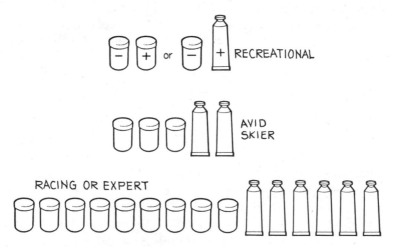

Most touring skiers need only two convenient wide-range waxes; more avid skiers will have a selection of five or so to better match a range of snow conditions. Experts and racers opt for a full selection to attain maximum waxed ski performance.

Waxing waxless

Although they usually grip well, many waxless skis have relatively poorer glide, especially on cold, granular, or wet snows. Special paraffin glider waxes are now available to improve the glide of waxless ski bases. They usually are available in aerosol-applicator cans and are applied to base tips and tails, ahead of and behind the waxless grip section.

A word to the wise

Learning how to wax is part of learning how to ski on waxable skis. The *how-to* of waxing is then beyond the scope of this book. But the art of waxing can be summed up in eight rules, guides to successful waxing:

1. Select one brand of wax, readily available where you live or ski, and learn it well; follow the manufacturer's directions.

2. Always check snow conditions before you wax. Note temperature, moisture in air, and snow type (new, old, settled).

3. Apply wax evenly and rub or spread it out well.

4. Use several thin layers: the more layers, the better the grip, but too many layers reduce glide.

5. Soft wax grips better than hard wax but also glides less well. A hard wax is a good base for a softer wax, but not vice versa.

6. Experiment with each wax you use until you know it well. When in doubt, use different numbers of layers of waxes you know well, instead of changing to waxes or brands with which you have no experience.

7. Learn Celsius (Centigrade) temperatures. They are handy for waxing: plus degrees usually mean wet snow, minus usually mean dry snow, and zero means the borderline.

8. "Dry skis" is a maxim. Wet skis hold wax poorly. Moisture in wood bases destroys bases and skis.

ACCESSORIES

Accessories, the tools of waxing, make it easier. Just as there are three categories of waxing, ranging from the simple and convenient to the complete and more complex, there are three groups of accessories, ranging from those that all who wax should have, to those that only the most thorough of waxers need.

Basic waxing tools: Ski scrapers and waxing corks are available in many types, both separate and as combined scraper-corks.

Scrapers are the minimum must of waxing tools.

One of each, or a combi-unit, is the minimum of tools that all waxers need. Corks, as the name implies, were once made of natural cork. Plastic foam corks are now common and, in many cases, are better for rubbing out waxes than are natural corks.

Supplementing the basics: Pocket waxing thermometers help you to judge snow conditions correctly.

Lint-free wiping tissue, such as the variety of trade-named tissues available from wax manufacturers, is ideal for wiping when cleaning or tarring skis. It's also handy for polishing glide waxes and hard waxes.

Waxing irons are a must for preparing plastic ski bases and warming-in hard waxes. Most are convenient hand-held units consisting of a solid rectangular aluminum block fixed to an insulating handle, designed so the block may easily be heated with a torch flame.

Waxing torches are used for warming-in base preparations on both plastic and wood-based skis, removing old wax, drying wet skis prior to waxing, and heating waxing irons. Almost all torches now available are fueled by liquid propane or butane gas.

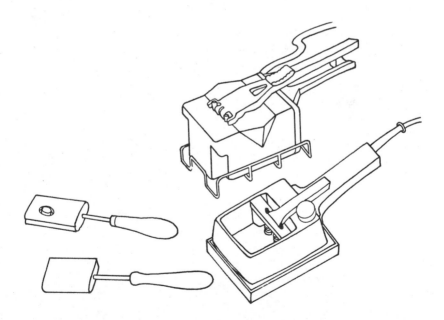

Typical waxing irons: left – small, hand-held irons, to be heated with a torch; right – electric waxing irons, with thermostatic control, wax reservoir, and dispenser mechanism.

Waxing torches aid waxing and cleaning.

Hand cleaners are special wax-dissolving creams, usually available in tubes. These cleaners should not be used on skis, as they contain oils that repel wax.

For complete waxing: In addition to the basic corks, scrapers, and supplementary accessories, the complete waxer—such as a racer, coach, or ski instructor—will usually have

—wax kits: hinged-cover boxes that resemble tool kits or attache cases. Supplied by the major wax makers, they hold all waxing needs neatly in place.

—waxing horses: collapsible stands that firmly clamp skis, bases up, at a height convenient for waxing. Special ski vises, which can

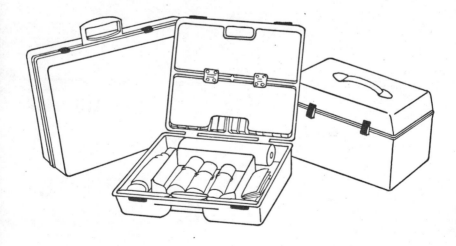

Wax kits hold all waxing needs.

be clamped to a table or workbench, are also available; they hold skis for waxing, cleaning, or binding mountings.

—electric waxers: special, thermostatically controlled waxing irons, with a reservoir for holding melted wax and a dispenser for applying wax to ski bases. They are most used in paraffin base preparation and glide waxing of plastic racing ski bases.

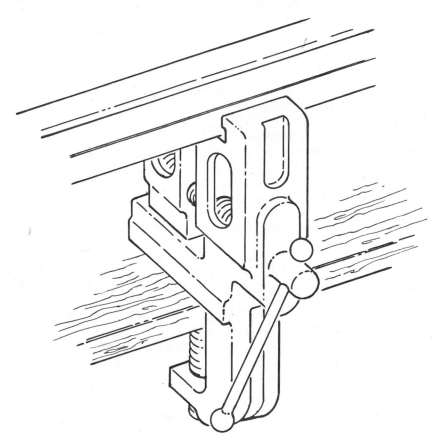

Ski vises clamp skis firmly for waxing or repair.

10   OTHER PARAPHERNALIA

Above and beyond the basics, there are many items that can add convenience, utility, or safety to cross-country skiing. The array of paraphernalia available may be, in fact, larger than that of ski equipment itself.

Some items, like tents, compasses, freeze-dried foods and cooking gear, are common to all outdoor activities and are described in detail in many outdoor handbooks and in the catalogs of wilderness and outdoor outfitters. A few categories of accessories, designed specifically for use by cross-country skiers, are described in this chapter.

First, skiers seldom travel without some baggage. For loads that exceed the capacity of pockets, skiers carry *packs* or pull *pulks*. Avid touring skiers and cross-country ski racers build skiing muscle strength off-season on *roller skis*. Finally, all skiers venturing away from maintained and patrolled trails should carry *skiing emergency gear*.

PACKS

Most skiers agree that it's easier to ski without a pack, any pack. Skiing movements are freer when there's less to wear and less to carry. But skiers often carry packs, for either convenience or necessity. Good skiing packs carry loads well while affording the skier as much packless skiing freedom as possible.

Many backpacking packs, although excellent for on-foot packing, are difficult to use and sometimes unwieldy when carried on skis. For instance, larger backpacking packframes that extend well above shoulder level can be so loaded as to carry weight too high for good skiing stability, and can be dangerous in a skiing fall.

Packs suitable for skiing classify primarily according to size and load capacity: mini-packs for convenience packing, day packs for day tours, and tour packs for longer tours, such as overnights.

Mini-packs

Mini-packs are small, frameless packs designed to carry wax, a lunch, a camera, and the other small odds and ends needed on shorter tours. They are more comfortable and convenient than stuffing items into parka pockets and come in two varieties: fanny packs and mini-knapsacks.

MINI-PACK

DAY-PACK

TOUR PACK

Packs for all touring needs.

Fanny packs strap around the waist with a wide belt, have as many as three compartments, and have amazing capacity for their size. The fanny pack moves well with the skier; so well, in fact, that it has sometimes been used by racers to carry wax in races run under difficult snow conditions. Fanny packs can be spun around in front for easy access.

Mini-knapsacks for skiing are broad and thin to distribute the load over and close to the back. Most models have two or more compartments and can comfortably carry about twice as much as a fanny pack. Mini-knapsacks also come in small sizes for small children, with capacities about equal to those of adult fanny packs.

Day and touring packs

Unlike mini-packs, which are primarily for convenience on shorter tours, day and touring packs are designed to carry the necessities for day tours or longer tours, such as overnights. A well-designed day pack or touring pack should

—fit the body well and not bounce or shift. It should move with, not against the skier

—place load close into the body so as not to upset skier on downhills or turns

—be narrow enough to allow full, free arm movement past the body in the cross-country poling movements

—have a waist and/or sternum (chest) strap, so the pack will stay in place and not jiggle or sway with body movement or ride up onto the neck or over the head in a fall, which may cause injury

—have internal pockets, dividers, or compartments so packed items stay in place and can be quickly located

—have shoulder and waist straps easily adjustable while pack is being worn

—have the top of the shoulder straps attached high on the pack to prevent pack swaying with skier's stride

—be waterproof and have a double flap or flap-over-drawstring closure. Flap should have a pocket for easy access to often-used items, such as map and compass

—be as light as possible.

The major difference between touring packs and day packs is size: touring packs are designed to carry larger loads. Also, touring packs usually have more features than day packs, as suits their use on longer tours. They may have straps for carrying skis, ice axes, or crampons; detachable pockets; adjustable size sacks; bivouac sack extensions; or more sack compartments than day packs.

Picking packs

Like ski equipment, you should pick the pack that best suits you and your packing needs. Start selection with an evaluation of use and consider your height and the weight and volume you wish to carry. Then consider specific features or designs.

Use: Frequent, convenient use for shorter tours dictates the choice of a mini-pack. Most cross-country skiers who prefer to carry more on their outings opt for day packs. When in doubt, it's best to select a larger day pack, as a partly full larger pack always carries more comfortably than an overstuffed, smaller mini-pack. Touring packs are ideal for packing the necessities for overnight trips but are, in general, too large for comfortable use on day trips with lighter loads.

Size: Packs come in different sizes, often with frames and/or sacks suited to different body heights. Select according to your height, so the pack carries comfortably and according to the weight you intend to carry.

The basic design of packs falls into two main categories suitable for skiing use: *frame packs* and *frameless packs*.

Frame packs are essentially sacks attached to an external frame or containing an internal frame. In the external frame type, webbing attached to the frame supports the pack against the back, and shoulder, waist, and chest straps attach to the frame and/or the pack sack. In the internal frame type, the sack rides against the back, and straps attach to the sack and sometimes to the frame.

Frame packs are generally at least somewhat adjustable for height by moving the shoulder-strap attaching points. Loading is far less critical and they do provide ventilation. Frame packs are, of course, self-supporting whether empty or full. Most frames are welded, making them rigid and vulnerable to breaking in a tumbling fall. Nonwelded frames can be more flexible and some are infinitely adjustable over a wide range. The major disadvantage of frame packs is that if a pack is improperly selected and/or adjusted, it may be uncomfortable to carry.

Frameless packs are contoured to fit closely against the body. Shoulder, waist, and chest straps are attached directly to the pack sack and hold it firmly against the back.

Frameless packs are usually lighter than frame packs and are easily rolled or folded for storage or carrying when empty. Size is particularly important: the upper attachment of the shoulder straps should be just even with the shoulders when the waist strap is cinched firmly just above the hips. Few frameless packs offer any vertical adjustment.

The major disadvantage of packs without frames is that they fit the back so closely that ventilation can be cut off, trapping perspiration against the skier's back and in clothing. Even the packs themselves and some of their contents can become saturated. Another disadvantage is that care and practice are needed in packing, removing, and replacing contents to keep a hard or sharp item from digging into your back.

Some frameless packs have wood, plastic, or aluminum stays; the latter can be bent for individual comfort. Packs with stays offer most of the advantages of frame packs, except for adjustability.

Loading packs

The general rule in on-foot backpacking is to carry heavy items high, a maxim related to the custom in many Eastern and African societies of carrying large loads on the head. This rule assumes a

Weight high, a good rule for backpacking on foot, places excess load on upper back of skier.

walking position, with the back vertical. In skiing, where the upper body inclines forward, high loads are inadvisable, both because they unduly load the back and because they upset skier balance.

The general rule for loading packs for skiing is to place heavy items close to the back. Place often-used items on top. In packing frameless packs, avoid all hard edges against the back; pad first with a sweater or folded towel. Place frequently used items—such as ski wax, sunglasses, suntan lotion, and so on—in outside pockets for ready access.

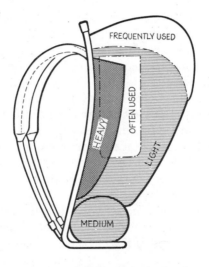

For skiing, pack heavy items lower, close to the back.

The better packs, particularly those with frames, feature padded waist straps designed to transfer weight from the shoulders to the hips. Not only is the weight kept lower by "hip suspension," but the shoulders and upper body have greater freedom for skiing motions. To take advantage of this, "hunch" your shoulders somewhat as you cinch the waist strap/belt snugly. Then relay your shoulders and you'll feel the weight transfer. Next, adjust each shoulder strap until the pack will not sway during skiing motions.

PULKS

A *pulk* is a boat-shaped runnerless sled, developed from the reindeer-drawn sleds (*bul'ka* in Lappish, *pulka* in Swedish) used for centuries by the nomadic Lapps of the arctic regions of Northern Europe. Like toboggans, pulks ride directly on the snow, but otherwise they differ.

The toboggan developed from the bark-and-skin runnerless sled of the American Indian and is usually flat, with a front upturn and a flat tail. Pulks have sides, like a boat, and often have a pram-like bow and stern, as the Lapps built both their river boats and their sleds in the same manner. Like the Viking ships of the time, the Lapp river boats and pulks were built of overlapping planks, running fore-and-aft on a frame, and thus were among the earliest of clinker-built boats.

The original Lappish pulks were primarily passenger sleds. The Lapps also made heavier cargo sleds (*ahkio* in Lappish, *ackja* in Swedish) resembling pulks, but fashioned from hollowed-out logs, like dugout boats used in the tropics.

Modern pulks are available in a range of types and sizes, suited to various purposes, loads, and speeds. Lightest and most common are kiddie-pulks, over-snow baby carriages intended to be pulled by a skier. At the heavy end of the pulk range are cargo pulks, sometimes called akia sleds, designed to be drawn by dog teams or snowmobiles. Some models of pulk are designed for pure speed, such as those in competitive Nordic dog-sled racing, a sport where a cross-country ski racer skis along behind a dog-drawn pulk. The range of models is shown in the table.

Materials: Most pulk shells are molded of fiberglass-reinforced polyester plastic. Covers are made of heavy nylon duck. Most fittings are aluminum; parts subjected to extreme stress, such as rear brakes, are usually made of steel. Most draw shafts are made

TYPES OF PULKS

| Type and use | Drawn by | Typical size | | Maximum load, pounds |
		Length, inches	Weight, pounds	
Kiddie, oversnow baby carriage	One skier	50	12	100
Transport and dog sled racing	One or two dogs or skiers	48-56	11-16	60-130
Rescue and transport	Two skiers or dog team	73-79	24-28	200-280
Cargo	Dog team or snowmobile	90	33	400

Kiddie pulk is an over-snow baby carriage.

"RUDOLF WITH YOUR NOSE SO BRIGHT, WON'T YOU DRAW MY PULK TONIGHT?"

The origin of pulks and akia sleds is unknown, but they were first mentioned in the accounts of travelers on the fur trade route from Great Bulgar to the White Sea, some two hundred years before it was obliterated by the expanding Mongol Empire of Genghis Khan. They were next mentioned, along with skis, in the writings of sixteenth- and seventeenth-century scholars traveling to the arctic regions.

Foremost of these works is the travelogue *Opera Lapponia* by Johan Scheffer, a professor of mathematics and language at the University of Uppsala, published in 1674 upon his return from his travels among the Lapps. The book, translated from the original Latin into several European languages, contained lengthy descriptions and woodcuts of skiers and reindeer-drawn pulks. Most complete of these books was the edition of 1682, published in Amsterdam, in The Netherlands.

So if the Santa Claus of today were as scholarly as he is jolly, his reindeer-drawn sleigh would probably be a pulk, as he is, after all, a Dutchman: *Santa Claus* is a contraction of the Dutch *Sint Nikolaas,* for Saint Nicholas. Although Santa's *sleigh* is the superior word for rhyme in children's Christmas songs, there's no record of runner-type sleighs ever

of fiberglass tubing or tonkin, but some are made of aluminum. Dog harnesses and draw belts for skiers are usually leather or nylon webbing.

Design: Aside from being strong and easily drawn, good pulks should be as stable as possible to resist capsizing like a displacement-hull sailboat. The best shell cross-section is one with sides that slope outward so a tipped pulk will right itself. Kiddie pulks should have a back support for safety and comfort in carrying children up to five years old. Kiddie pulks and rescue pulks should have structural members or attachments that function as roll bars, just in case the pulk does capsize with a passenger. In kiddie pulks, roll protection is often built into the windshield and into the back support. Most pulks have runners, either molded into or attached to their shells. These runners are small, seldom over an inch in width: they aid tracking and withstand abrasion but do not support the pulk—unlike the runners of a Yukon-type dogsled.

ROLLER SKIS

Roller skis are skate-like devices used to simulate cross-country skiing on paved surfaces. They are used by racers and serious cross-country skiers to train skiing muscles and reflexes, off season or away from snow.

---

being drawn by reindeer. Some unknown artist's imagination looms stronger than historical fact. But change is always possible. One could even sing: "Rudolf don't you sulk, Santa wants you to draw his pulk."

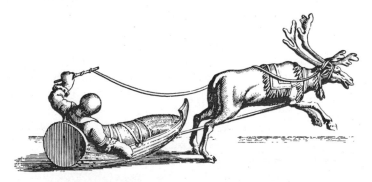

Woodcut of Lapp in reindeer-drawn pulk, from Scheffer's Opera Lapponia, *London edition of 1704.*

Roller skis attach to the feet with cross-country bindings and boots. Most models now available consist of a laminated wood or rectangular aluminum body, usually about 48 mm wide, about the same width as many light-touring skis. Most roller skis are fitted with one forward and two rear wheels. Wheels average five inches in diameter and are fitted with hard rubber tires, although larger wheels, with pneumatic-type tires, are available on some models. A pair of roller skis with bindings weighs about 6½ pounds, more than double the weight of a pair of racing skis with bindings. Roller skis are relatively short: current models average just slightly over three feet in length.

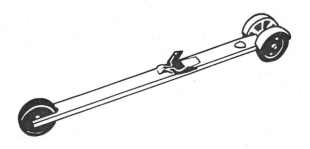

Roller skis resemble giant roller skates.

Most roller skis have a ratchet mechanism built into the hubs of one or more wheels to permit forward and prevent backward roll, to simulate on-snow grip and glide. Models are available with the ratchet on the front or on the rear wheels. Racers usually prefer models with the ratchet on the rear wheels because in the diagonal stride backward resistance stops as soon as the rear wheels lift off the ground. This gives a closer approximation of the grip of racing skis and aids racers in practicing short, explosive kicks.

Some roller skis feature a brake mechanism, activated by foot or pole pressure. Brakes are useful if you roller ski where there are steeper downhills. Otherwise, roller skiing should be limited to flat, uphill, and very gradual downhill stretches, as falling on pavement is far more hazardous than falling on snow.

Roller skiing can be done using ordinary ski poles, usually with the baskets removed. Pole length is about the same as used on snow, as pole tips do not sink in and most roller skis place the foot about three inches above the pavement, the height the basket would be relative to the pole tip on snow.

Roller skiing simulates skiing.

However, roller skiing is best done using poles specially designed for the purpose. Roller ski poles have standard ski pole grips and wrist loops and usually have sturdy shafts of aluminum alloy to better resist damage in case of a fall. Tips are usually sharpened, sintered carbide, to bite into pavement surfaces, and are set in spring-loaded ferrules to absorb partially the shock of poling on hard surfaces. For racers, this shock-absorbing feature is particularly advisable, as prolonged roller-ski training using standard poles may sometimes damage wrist and elbow joints due to the repeated shocks of pole tips striking the hard pavement surface.

Caution: Always check traffic regulations before buying or using roller skis, as local or state ordinances may restrict their use on roads, sidewalks, or parking lots. For safety, roller skis are best used away from all other traffic.

EMERGENCY SKIING GEAR

You should always take emergency equipment along on longer tours, especially where you are on your own, away from marked and maintained trail networks.

Most emergency equipment is similar to that which should be taken along on any tour of comparable length under the same weather conditions, whether on foot, snowshoes, or skis: extra clothing, windproof outer garments, first aid kit, emergency food, whistle to call attention, sun glasses or goggles, flashlight or headlamp, and a sharp knife. Wilderness skiers and ski mountaineers should add items suited to the remoteness of their trips in rugged terrain, such as avalanche cord, emergency fuel, and stove.

Touring skiers should take along extra items specifically designed for skiing emergencies: one or more emergency ski tips and an emergency snow spade.

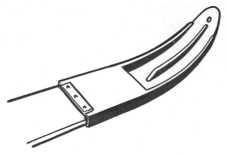

A spare ski tip is a must for wilderness touring.

If skis, particularly wood skis, break in use, they usually break at or near the tip. Emergency ski tips, designed to fit over the broken front of a ski, allow you to keep moving. Most emergency ski tips are now made of plastic and are available in two widths, one to fit light-touring skis and a broader model to fit touring and ski mountaineering skis. The tips simply push onto the ski and are held firmly in place by spring-loaded metal teeth.

The lightweight shovels are intended for emergency and rescue work, such as for digging a snow bivouac or assisting in an avalanche search operation. Most have aluminum alloy blades that fit to detachable wood handles, or have a hinged handle, like an Army entrenching tool. Although intended to be packed for ski emergencies, these shovels are also useful for digging out snowed-in cars.

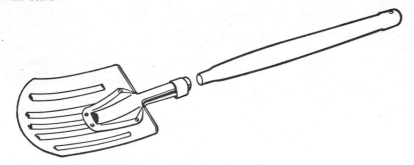

An emergency snow shovel, the skier's friend on tours.

11 SKI JUMPING EQUIPMENT

Even for cross-country skiers who will never jump, some information on the subject is useful. As a cross-country skier, you may become interested in cross-country ski racing. And as major meets are often Nordic, you may therefore be exposed to ski jumping, which is on the upswing worldwide.

Ski jumping differs from all other forms of skiing in two respects. First, it is a competitive event only: it has no recreational equivalent. Second, flight is the major feature of a ski jumping performance. This means that ski jumping equipment is designed for best in-flight performance, as well as for best on-snow performance on the inrun of a jump before flight and on the outrun after landing. Like the equipment for other forms of skiing, ski jumping gear is divided into the categories of skis, boots, bindings, clothing, and waxing. Ski jumpers do not use poles.

International Ski Federation (FIS) regulations govern all equipment used in international ski jumping meets. Because ski jumping is a competition-only sport, jumping equipment is almost always made to conform to the FIS regulations.

SKIS

Jumping skis are different from any other type of ski, as suits their special purpose. They are designed to track as straight as possible on the inrun of a ski jump, and they have a relatively soft tip flex that "floats" the tips easily over uneven parts of the inrun track. They have relatively large bottom surfaces for best aerodynamic lift in flight. They are stronger than any other type of ski, to absorb the shock of landing. Their flexural stiffness distribution is designed to put as much of the base as possible on the snow after landing, to provide the jumper with the best possible ski control. Ski forebodies are designed to absorb the shock of the transition from the landing slope to the outrun.

FIS regulations as of 1979 governed dimensions only: *length*— 270 cm maximum; *widths*—115 mm maximum width, 60 mm minimum waist width; *heights*—30 mm minimum shovel upturn height, 10 mm maximum tail upturn height.

Length: Jumping skis are longer than cross-country or Alpine skis. For instance, an average 5 foot 11 inch ski jumper will most often use 250-cm jumping skis, 40 cm longer than the 210-cm skis used by average cross-country ski racers of the same height. The imprinted length of almost all jumping skis is the material length (measured along the ski base). The tips of jumping skis turn up less than those of cross-country skis, so there is very little difference between the various methods of ski length measurement that could be used, less than one centimeter for a 250-cm jumping ski.

Width and side profile: Jumping skis are broader than all other types of skis. Waist widths now average 88 mm, broader than the shovel widths of most modern Alpine downhill racing skis. Jumping ski shovel widths are usually slightly over 100 mm, tail widths slightly less than 100 mm. This combination of widths gives the skis a pronounced sidecut, a little over 6 mm (¼ in.) on each side. This profile aids tracking at high ski speeds, which, on larger ski jumps, may be 60 mph or more—ski jumpers move faster than cars can be driven legally on U.S. highways!

Camber and flexural stiffness: Compared to all other types of skis, jumping skis have very little camber height and low overall flex: they are relatively soft. Placed base-to-base, a good pair of jumping skis can easily be squeezed together between the thumb and fingers of one hand. Tips are softer than tails, a flexural stiffness distribution designed to keep ski bases on the snow on the inrun and outrun as well as aid in absorbing the shock of landing.

Construction: Almost all modern jumping skis use a sandwich construction of fiberglass on a laminated wood or wood-foam plastic core. Bases are usually of a high-density polyethylene and have four or more tracking grooves for maximum tracking stability. For best in-flight aerodynamics, jumpers prefer that ski balance points lie behind midpoints. Therefore, the tail sections of ski cores usually are weighted, most often with lead. Weight size and placement

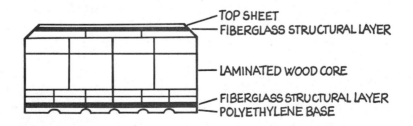

TOP SHEET
FIBERGLASS STRUCTURAL LAYER

LAMINATED WOOD CORE

FIBERGLASS STRUCTURAL LAYER
POLYETHYLENE BASE

Cross-section of typical modern fiberglass sandwich-type jumping ski construction.

180

vary with ski model but typically average 7 ounces of lead just ahead of the ski tail.

Selecting jumping ski length

Jumping ski length depends on a ski jumper's height, weight, and strength and on the size of the ski jumping hills. In general, taller, heavier, and stronger ski jumpers will use longer jumping skis than shorter, lighter jumpers. Ski jumping hills are classified according to their norm point lengths, measured from the lip of the jump, along the surface of the snow, to the norm point, between the convex and concave transition curve. Most ski jumps are designed so the maximum possible jump length is the norm point length (designated "P") plus about ten percent. Ski jumps with P up to 50 meters are classified as *small hills;* those with P of 60 to 70 meters as *normal hills;* those with P of 80 to 90 meters as *large hills;* and those with P of 125 meters as *ski flying hills.* In general, children jumping on small hills use shorter skis than young poeple or adults jumping on larger hills. However, since ski jumping is an athletic event that can be viewed as a relative of acrobatics, a ski jumper's balance and "feel" are as important as other factors involved in selecting skis. The general guidelines for jumping ski length are shown in the table.

GUIDELINES FOR SELECTING JUMPING SKI LENGTHS

Jumper age	Size of ski jumping hill, norm point length (P) in *meters*	Recommended jumping ski length		
8-14-year-olds	*Small hills* (P up to 50 m)	Fingertips of upraised arm should just reach start of shovel upturn		
15-17-year-olds	*Normal hills* (P = 60 to 70 m) and *Large hills* (P = 80 to 90 m)	*Height* 5'7" 5'9" 5'11"		*Ski length* 240 cm 245 cm 250 cm
18-year-olds and older	*Normal hills* (P = 60 to 70 m) *Large hills* (P = 80 to 90 m) *Ski flying hills* (P = 125 m)	No general recommendations, as senior jumpers usually select on basis of personal preference. Most common lengths now used: 245, 250, 252, 255 cm		

BOOTS

Jumping boots differ from other types of ski boots because their purpose is different. In general, jumping boots resemble over-ankle ski touring boots, except that they are considerably higher and stiffer and have a pronounced forward lean. Collars are high in the rear for sturdy calf support when the jumper crouches on the inrun and to aid rapid tip rise just after take-off. Soles are designed to bend easily, hinge-like, under the ball of the foot, to ease in-flight forward lean. Most boots now have two separate sets of laces: the main laces that close the upper around the foot, and an upper lace for adjusting fit and tension around the lower calf of the leg.

Almost all boots are padded and have leather uppers Norwegian-welt-sewn to laminated leather-rubber sandwich soles. Sole profiles resemble, but do not necessarily conform to, the Nordic Norm used for cross-country boots.

BINDINGS

Jumping bindings resemble cable-type ski touring bindings and comprise a toepiece, a cable with a heel spring, a front throw with a

Jumping boots are high and have a pronounced forward lean.

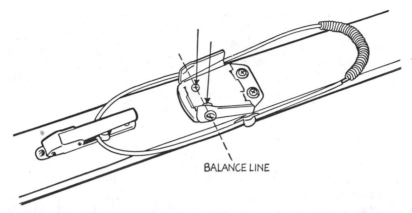

BALANCE LINE

Cable-type jumping bindings mount with forward two screws on ski balance line.

mechanism for adjusting cable tension, and two side hooks to hold the cable under the binding ears.

Most bindings are designed to be adjustable in mounting, to custom fit the soles of the boots fitted, and are made of steel for strength.

Most jumpers prefer to mount rubber *heel wedges* behind the bindings to lift boot heels 1 to 5 cm (up to 2 in.) off the ski. Wedging eases a jumper's squat in the active, prejump position and aids rapid ski tip rise after take-off. The size of the wedge used depends on the individual ski jumper's strength and ankle mobility.

Mounting bindings: Ski jumpers need a relatively long portion of their skis under their bodies when in flight for best aerodynamic lift and long ski jumps. Therefore, jumping skis are balanced at a point 10 to 15 cm (4 to 6 in.) behind the midpoint of the ski. Typical for a current-production fiberglass jumping ski is a

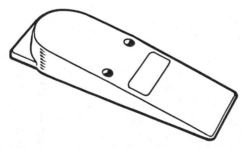

Rubber heel wedge mounts on ski to elevate boot heel for additional forward lean.

balance point 114 cm from the tail of a 250 cm ski. Bindings are usually mounted with the forward two of the four mounting screws on the ski balance line. Cable sidehitches are mounted just under the rear edges and flush with the binding ears. The cable front throw is mounted ahead of the binding toepiece, at a location that permits cable tensions to be adjusted from taut to completely loose with a boot in the binding.

CLOTHING

Ski jumpers wear one-piece suits, helmets, and gloves, similar to those used by downhill ski racers. Present (1979) FIS regulations govern suits and helmets.

Suits: The FIS regulations for ski jumping suits are intended to promote safety and assure fair competition.

For safety, ultra-slick, plasticized materials are not permitted in suits. In falls, the slick materials are extremely dangerous, because they are so smooth that a fallen jumper skids on the snow out of control, taking far too long to stop.

In ski jumping, the body of the jumper is a critical factor in the aerodynamic lift required for longer jumps. Part of the skill of ski jumping lies in the jumper being able to arch the body for best aerodynamic effect. A good aerodynamic cross-section can also be achieved by other means, such as by allowing air trapped in a jumper's suit to billow the back up, forming an airfoil like an airplane wing. This requires that portions of the back of the suit be airtight. The FIS has outlawed this type of suit to ensure that the most skilled jumpers, not those with the most cleverly designed suits, achieve best results.

Therefore, the present FIS regulations, in force through the 1980 Winter Olympics, stipulate that ski jumping suit material must not be airtight but must allow at least 50 liters of air passage per minute per square meter of fabric, at a pressure difference corresponding to 10 mm of water column. The same material must be used for all parts of the suit, and the suit back must have an air permeability equal to or greater than that of the front of the suit.

Helmets: The FIS now requires that helmets be worn by jumpers in all international ski jump meets to reduce the chances of head injury in falls. The helmets approved by the FIS resemble those used in downhill ski racing. Like many motorcycle and hockey helmets, ski jumping helmets are usually made of ABS plastic, lined with expanded foam plastic, and held in place by a chin strap fitted with an impact-resistant chin protector. Ski jumping helmets are now available in six sizes, to fit child, youth, and senior jumpers.

WAXING

Waxing for ski jumping is similar to waxing for Alpine ski racing. Most ski jumpers prefer hot waxing, followed by scraping and polishing, techniques also used by downhill ski racers. Ski jumpers use the same waxes as Alpine ski racers but usually select waxes for conditions 4° to 5°C (7° to 9°F) warmer than an Alpine ski racer would for the same snow conditions. Ski jumpers "wax warmer" for two reasons:

First, although jumping gear is heavy (a pair of 250-cm jumping skis with bindings and wedges plus a pair of size 8 ski jumping boots weighs approximately 25 pounds), jumping skis place about 40 percent more area on the snow than the broadest and longest Alpine skis, so ski pressure is less.

Second, on larger ski jumping hills (norm point length P of 80 meters or more), take-off and landing speeds are high, 55 to 60 mph or more. These high speeds produce more frictional heating under the skis than would be the case for most Alpine skiing, except downhill racing, under the same conditions.

GLOSSARY

Like most activities, Nordic (cross-country) skiing has its own special vocabulary that describes the activity and its equipment and apparel. Here are the terms most used. Definitions or applications not pertaining to Nordic skiing are not given. All trade names and trademarks are assumed to be registered.

ABS: Trade name for Acrylonitrile Butadiene Styrene, a plastic used in ski top sheets, ski bases, binding parts, and ski jumping helmets.

Acrylic: (1) Polymethacrylimide, a foam plastic used in ski cores. (2) Polyacrylonitrile fibers or fabric, used in clothing.

Active surface: Portion of ski base active in contact with snow; usually denotes the contact length, but sometimes only the midsection of base waxed for grip, or containing waxless base pattern.

Adikiel: Trade name for grooveless ski base, with raised keel.

Aerobic: Literally "with air"; describes body processes requiring oxygen.

Aerobic capacity: A measure of the ability to perform aerobic work over longer periods of time. Often expressed as maximum oxygen uptake.

Afterbody: Rear half of ski, behind ski balance line.

Agility: In skiing, the ability to use body flexibility efficiently.

Aircraft aluminum: Aluminum alloy, usually containing magnesium and manganese, used in ski bindings and ski poles.

Akia sled: Large pulk, usually used for rescue or cargo transport.

Alpine skiing: Recreational and competitive downhill skiing, developed in Europe's Alps in the 1920s.

AMU: Abbreviation for *atomic mass units*, used to express molecular weight, most often of base plastics; written *amu*.

Anaerobic: Literally "without air"; describes body processes that can function without oxygen. Sometimes termed "oxygen debt."

Anaerobic capacity: A measure of the body's capability to perform muscular work over and above the limit set by maximum oxygen uptake.

Anorak: Lightweight shell parka, usually with a hood.

Aramid: Synthetic fiber used in structural layers of skis, acronym for *ar*omatic poly*amide*.

Arm trainers: Various devices used by ski racers in off-season arm training; provide resistance against arms in poling movements.

Arnite: Trade name for type of polyacetate plastic, used in ski bindings.

Backslip: Skis grip snow poorly and slip backwards.

Bail: Clamp-down piece on toe binding, holds boot sole down with or against pins.

Base: (1) Running surface of a ski. (2) Snow under surface snow.

Base preparation: Compounds or process of their application—tars for wood ski bases, paraffin waxes for plastic ski bases.

Base wax: Wax used "under" final wax to increase durability.

Basket: Disk attached near bottom of ski pole to prevent its sinking into snow.

Biathlon: Competitive skiing event combining cross-country ski racing and rifle marksmanship.

Bib knickers: Knickers with high bib front and shoulder straps.

Binding: Device, mounted on ski, to attach boot to ski.

Binding jig: Jig for locating holes drilled for mounting bindings on skis.

Boat: Ski side profile, waist broader than tip or tail.

Bowed: Ski base convex instead of flat, center higher than edges.

Box: Synthetic ski construction in which load-carrying material forms a box enclosing core on all four sides.

Cable binding: Binding with toe piece and cable or strap around boot heel, used on heavier wilderness skis and on jumping skis.

Calorie: Physiological unit, used to express the heat output of the body and the energy values of foods.

Camber: Arch of the middle of a ski above its tip and tail.

Camber pocket: Horizontal length under portion of camber curve not yet flattened out when ski is weighted.

Camber resistance: Force necessary to flatten out a ski's camber.

Camber stiffness: Stiffness distributed over ski's camber, uniformly or nonuniformly, usually expressed as force required to straighten out portion of camber in question.

Camel walk: See Passgang.

Cangoran: Trade name for synthetic leather comprising four layers, used in boot uppers.

Carbon fiber: Filaments of carbon, used in ski poles and structural layers of skis, usually encased in epoxy resin.

Cemented boot: Boot in which sole is bonded to upper with adhesive, usually in a process involving pressure and heat.

Chord length: Straight-line distance between ski tip and tail.

Christie: Short for Christiania, after the older name of Oslo; describes side-slipping phase of some downhill ski turns.

CISM: Conseil International Militaire du Sport—organizers of military ski racing.

Citizens' race: Cross-country ski race for recreational skiers, usually mass start.

Clo: Unit used to express insulating value of clothing.

Clog: To collect snow and ice up, used of ski bases.

Collar: Strip of material fastened around top opening of a boot, often padded for comfort.

Combined: In Nordic skiing, competition combining 15-km cross-country ski racing and ski jumping on a 70-meter hill.

Competition: Class of cross-country racing equipment intended for competition use only.

Composite base: Waxless ski base of composite material, usually particles for grip, angled backwards, set in plastic for glide.

Composites: Manufactured materials comprising resin, filler, and synthetic fibers, used in ski structural layers, pole shafts, and boot and binding parts.

Conduction: Transfer of heat by direct contact.

Contact length: Length of ski base in contact with underlying surface when ski is not weighted.

Convection: Transfer of heat through circulation of air.

Corduroy: Ribbed fabric, usually of cotton or cotton-synthetic blend, usually heavy.

Core: Central part of wood or synthetic ski, between or encased by structural layers; gives ski shape.

Cork: A block of material, originally natural cork, now usually foam plastic, used to rub and polish ski wax on ski base.

Corn: Large-grained snow, produced by settling and repeated freezing and thawing.

Cosmetics: External color, design, logos, lettering, etc., especially on skis, boots, and poles.

Counter: Piece of material inserted between lining and outside of boot upper to keep it stiff.

Course: Route followed by a ski race.

Crepe: Lightweight synthetic or synthetic-cotton fabric, usually stretch, often used in wind garments.

Cross-bonding: Production method for synthetic-fiber ski pole shaft tubing; fibers wound in crossing spirals around tube.

Cross-country: In common usage, the entirety of recreational ski touring and competitive cross-country ski racing. Strictly, the competitive form only.

Crust: Glazed snow surface, caused by freeze-thaw cycles.

Damping: How well a ski reduces or "deadens" vibration.

Day pack: Small backpack, used by skiers on day tours.

Delrin: Trade name for polyacetate plastic, used in ski bindings.

Denier: Number indicating size of silk and synthetic fiber filaments and yarns; equal to weight in grams of 9000 meters (9840 yards) of filament or yarn.

Diagonal stride: Stride in which opposite arm and leg move in unison, as in walking on foot.

Diamond glide: Trade name for diamond-pattern embossed waxless ski base.

DIN: Abbreviation, for German National Standards, originally for Deutsche Industrienorm, but now for all standards published by Deutsches Institut für Normung. DIN standards group 602 for Sports Equipment covers ski equipment.

Distance training: Endurance training, used by racers, aimed at building aerobic power.

Divinycell: Trade name for PVC foam plastic.

Double-box: Trade name for box-type ski structure comprising two boxes, one within the other.

Double camber: Geometric interpretation of modern ski camber where center section is stiffer than tip or tail sections.

Double poling: Gliding ski maneuver in which both arms move in unison, planting poles for forward thrust.

Dry-snow skis: Racing skis for use on dry snow, usually with relatively softer camber stiffness and high-density plastic base.

Duck: Close-woven, heavy fabric, usually cotton or cotton-synthetic, used for accessories such as mitten shells and gaiters.

Dynamic: In motion. Usually an adjective, such as *dynamic force,* a force due to motion.

Edge: Bottom outside edge of ski base, of material differing from rest of base.

Egg: Ultra-compact, crouching downhill ski position.

Electric waxer: Electrically heated waxing iron, usually with a reservoir for melted wax and a mechanism for dispensing wax directly onto ski base.

Endurance: The ability to perform prolonged work, such as in distance skiing, without fatigue.

Epoxy: A resin, used as an adhesive and as a binder for various synthetic fibers in skis and poles.

Ergometer cycle: A stationary cycle on which a subject pedals at a fixed speed against a fixed resistance. Used in measuring aerobic endurance.

Ethyl Vinyl Acetate (EVA): Flexible plastic that retains properties in cold, used for ski pole parts, especially baskets.

Evaporation: Process of converting water to vapor; requires heat.

Evaporative ability: Ability of a wet clothing fiber to allow moisture evaporation.

Fall-line: Shortest line directly down a hill.

Fartslek: From the Swedish; literally "speed game," a form of off-snow training for racing.

Fastex: Trade name for type of polyethylene ski base.

Ferrule: Tube fitting over bottom of ski pole, usually fitted with metal tip.

Fiberglass: Glass filaments, spun or thrown together, encased in a resin, often epoxy, to form structural layers of skis and ski pole shafts.

Fibre-tran: Trade name for synthetic pile, used for waxless ski bases.

FIS: Fédération Internationale de Ski—The International Ski Federation. Headquarters: Elfenstrasse 19, CH-3000 Bern 16, Switzerland.

Fishscale: Trademark for pattern-type waxless ski base having imbricated scales.

Flat ski: Ski held flat on snow in skiing, usually during a turn.

Fleece: Insulating boot lining, originally natural fleece, but now usually synthetic pile.

Flex: Bending properties of a ski or ski pole.

Flexibility: (1) Flex. (2) Measure of physical movement capability, such as how far a body part can bend.

Forebody: Front half of a ski ahead of the balance line.

Forward spring: Characteristic of a cross-country ski to spring upward and forward when unweighted.

Frame pack: Backpack with a detachable or internal frame.

Frameless pack: Backpack with no frame; may have removable stays.

Friction: Resistance between two surfaces to sliding over one another; when surfaces slide, friction produces heat.

Gaiter: Cloth covering around leg and boot at ankle; keeps snow out.

Glide: Property of a ski base to slide on snow.

Glider: Paraffin wax used on tip and tail section of ski bases for glide.

Gore-Tex: Trademark for microporous film, breathable and highly water repellent, used as laminate on fabrics.

Grafil: Trademark for carbon fiber, used in ski structural layers and in ski pole shafts.

Granular snow: Snow comprising large, coarse crystals.

Grip: (1) Property of a ski to bite into underlying snow. (2) The handle of a ski pole.

Groove: (1) Long, narrow indentation in ski base; aids tracking. (2) Indentation, often V-shaped, in bottom surface of boot heel; mates with device on ski. (3) Round indentation around outside of boot heel, to hold cable of cable-type binding.

Grundvalla: Swedish term for base wax.

Hair base: Waxless ski base; base irregularities comprise natural or synthetic fur, usually inset in strips or rectangles, nap backwards.

Hard wax: Wax for cold and dry to slightly wet snow.

Heel plate: Plate mounted on ski under boot heel, usually with features designed to hold weighted heel on ski.

Helanca: Trade name for process of producing elastic yarn for stretch fabrics from nylon fibers.

Herringbone: Uphill stride, skis spread to form a V; named for pattern left in snow.

Hickory: Strongest, most durable, heaviest wood used in wood skis and cores of synthetic skis. Often used for wood ski bases.

High-density: Usually applies to ski base plastic material; indicates relatively high material molecular weight.

Hobbling: Undesirable quality of excess clothing to restrict body movement at joints.

Honeycomb: Matrix of six-sided aluminum-foil cells resembling honeycomb, used in ski cores.

Hydrophilic: Having a strong affinity for water (attracting or absorbing water). Used to describe materials.

Hydrophobic: Having little or no affinity for water (repelling water). Used to describe materials.

Hypothermia: Subnormal body temperature that slows physiological processes and can result in death.

Hytrel: Trade name for type of polyamide plastic, used in racing boot soles.

Imbricated: Overlapping in sequence like roof tiles or shingles; describes type of waxless ski base pattern.

Imitation training: Movements performed on foot to imitate and thus teach skiing movements.

Impregnation: Waterproofing process for (1) apparel, (2) wood ski bases.

Imprinted length: Length stamped or printed on skis or poles.

Injected boot: Boot type; soles formed on uppers by injecting plastic into a mold.

Injected ski: Ski in which core is formed by plastic injected into mold holding top and bottom structural layers.

Insole: Inner sole of a boot.

Interval training: A series of intense, short exercise periods separated by rests. Used by racers in off-season training.

IOC: The International Olympic Committee.

ISO: International Standards Organization.

Keel: Grooveless ski base profile, with center elevated above edges, used on some models of racing skis.

Kevlar: Trademark for aramid fibers, used in ski structural layers.

Kick: As in walking, a backward thrusting toe push-off and leg extension that provides forward thrust in skiing strides.

Kicker: Slang. Grip wax applied in midsection of ski base.

Kick-glide performance: Ski performance characteristics of various cross-country ski strides with alternating kick and glide.

Kick turn: A stationary about-face turn performed by lifting and reversing direction of one ski, followed by the other ski.

Kiddie pack: Frame-type backpack with seat designed to carry small child in sitting position.

Klegecell: Trade name for PVC foam plastic.

Klister: Tacky, fluid cross-country wax preparations, for wet and/or settled snow.

Klister ski: Wet-snow ski: competition ski specifically designed for use on wet snow, with klister.

Klister-wax: Tacky, hard wax for conditions near freezing.

Knickers: Breeches gathered at the knee, usually with elastic or buckle strap.

Knitted fabric: Fabric produced by knitting, process using one strand of yarn where loops join yarn to adjacent row.

Kofix: Trade name for type of polyethylene ski base.

Krymp: Trade name for hydrophobic leather.

Langlauf: German for cross-country ski racing.

Lateral stability: The ability of a weighted boot heel to stay on a ski.

Light-touring: Class of cross-country ski equipment, closely resembling racing equipment but stronger and slightly heavier.

Light track: Illuminated cross-country trail or track.

Lignostone: Trade name, from Latin *lignum,* wood; beech wood compressed to half volume, used for edges on wood skis.

Low-density: Relatively low material molecular weight, usually applied to ski base plastics.

Lycra: Trade name for stretch fabric containing polyurethane fibers.

Material length: Length measured along base of ski from tip to tail.

Matrix: Material that bonds synthetic fibers in place, giving form to product, such as ski structural layer or pole shaft.

Mercerizing: Process of treating cotton yarn or fabric with caustic alkali under tension, increasing strength and affinity for dye; named after English inventor John Mercer (1850).

Mica: Trade name for composite-type waxless ski base comprising backward-slanting mica particles imbedded in plastic base material.

Mini-pack: Small convenience pack, usually a frameless knapsack or belt-type "fanny pack."

Mohair: Originally, coat or fleece of Angora goat. In ski making, hair strips or rectangles inlaid in a waxless ski base, nap pointing backwards.

Mortise core: Mortise-joined composite wood core, used in some synthetic skis.

Mountain: Strongest, heaviest category of cross-country ski equipment, intended for wilderness skiing and ski mountaineering.

Muscular fitness: Ability of the skeletal muscles to perform movements.

Natural stance: Natural erect body position, used in downhill skiing.

Negative base: Pattern-type waxless ski base where waxless pattern lies under level of base.

Nordic: (1) Geographic: Norway, Sweden, and Finland. (2) Recreational and competitive cross-country skiing, biathlon, ski jumping equipment and apparel.

Nordic Norm: Standard boot and toe binding widths and side angles, most common (1979-80) for recreational cross-country boots and bindings, superseded 1980 by ISO Standard.

Norm 38: Design of racing boots and bindings, patented and developed in Central Europe.

NSPS: National Ski Patrol System. U.S. ski rescue and first aid corps, originally for Alpine ski slopes, now with cross-country patrols.

Nylon: Originally trade name, but now accepted as generic term for type of polyamide plastic, used in parts of skis, poles, boots, and bindings, and in fiber form, in ski apparel.

Orienteering: Competitive event combining running on foot or skis with map and compass use.

Overboots: Flexible, pull-over boot covers, for added insulation and water repellency.

Overdistance: Distance training for racing, usually off-season on foot, over distance greater than competitive racing distance.

OWG: Olympic Winter Games, held leap years from 1924 on.

Oxford cloth: Twill-weave textured fabric, usually of cotton, used for parkas.

Oxygen debt: Anaerobic.

Oxygen uptake: Measure of a body's ability to supply oxygen to bodily processes.

Parallel turn: Downhill turn made with skis parallel throughout turn.

Paris Point system: European shoe and boot size system: size number is 1.5 times inside length in centimeters.

Parka: Long jacket, usually waterproof and windproof, with hood.

Passgang: Obsolete touring stride in which arm and leg on one side move in unison.

Pattern base: Waxless ski base where irregularities that grip comprise a regular pattern molded or machined into base material.

Penetrometer: Device for measuring water-repellency of fabrics and boot upper materials.

Perlon: Trade name for polyamide fiber.

Pile fabric: Fabric with fur-like nap, used in garment linings.

Pin: (1) Short peg projecting upwards from base plate of toe binding; engages recess in boot sole. (2) Transverse spike that holds grip on ski pole.

Pin binding: Toe binding comprising metal or plastic toepiece with pins projecting upwards to mate recesses in boot sole.

Pole set: The act of planting a pole in the snow.

Poling: Arm movements with poles that supply forward thrust.

Polyacrylonitrile fiber: Synthetic fibers; can be spun to resemble wool in garments.

Polyamide: Polymer plastic; used in boot soles and inserts, binding parts, and pole parts. In fiber form, used in woven and knitted fabrics, often stretch.

Polyester: Polymer plastic, used to bind fiberglass in pole shafts and pulk shells. In fiber form, used in combination with natural fibers to reduce fabric wrinkle.

Polyethylene (PE): Plastic derived from ethylene gas, used for ski bases.

Polymethacrylimide (PMI): White, light, rigid plastic foam used in ski cores.

Polypropylene (PP): Plastic derived from propane gas, used for ski bases; fibers used in fabrics for transport-type underwear.

Polystyrene (PS): Light but relatively weak foam plastic, used as a filler in ski cores.

Polyurethane (PU): Gray or black foam plastic, used for boot soles and ski cores, especially of injected type. Fiber used in stretch fabrics.

Polyvinyl chloride (PVC): Plastic derived from vinyl chloride; gray or white foam, used for ski core filler.

Poplin: Smooth-surfaced cotton or cotton-synthetic cloth, usually windproof and treated for water repellency, used in parkas, knickers, and accessories.

Positive base: Pattern-type waxless ski base where waxless pattern protrudes beyond the level of the base.

Powder: Light, dry snow, usually at low temperatures.

Pozi-drive: Trade name for fluted screwdrivers and screws used to mount bindings.

Pre-preg: Fiberglass cloth preimpregnated with epoxy.

Primus: Trade name for kerosene-fueled camping stoves and torches.

Projected length: Horizontal tip-to-tail length of ski resting on horizontal surface.

P-Tex: Trade name for type of polyethylene ski base.

Pulk: Kayak-shaped sled, riding directly on snow as does toboggan, used by skiers to transport loads, small children, or injured.

Pullover socks: Overboots.

Racing Norm: Standard for racing boots and bindings, superseded 1980 by ISO Standard.

Radiation: Direct heat transfer through space; example is process whereby sun warms body.

Railed: Ski base concave instead of flat, edges higher than center.

Relay: In cross-country ski racing, a four-man, 40-km race or a four-woman, 20-km race. Shorter relays or mixed men's and women's are run nationally in some countries.

Residual camber: Camber height remaining as camber curve flattens out due to applied force.

Resilience: (1) Ski or pole spring. (2) Part of muscular fitness.

Rhovyl: Trade name for PVC fibers used in clothing.

Rip-stop: Lightweight nylon fabric, usually coated, woven to resist tears and rips, used in sleeping bags and parka liners and in some lightweight parkas and windsuits.

Roller skis: Skatelike platforms that attach like skis to boots, for simulating ski movements, off-season, in training for racing.

Rough-out leather: Boot upper leather, either reversed top grain leather with rough inside out, or split leather with deliberately roughened outside.

Roving: Twisted, cleaned strand of fiber, prior to conversion into yarn.

Rucksack: Knapsack with a frame, suitable for skiing.

Sandwich ski: Wood or synthetic ski built up of several laminations bonded together in a sandwichlike fashion.

Scraper: Metal or plastic rectangle or blade, used to remove old wax or flatten bases.

Shaft: Tubular, straight part of a ski pole.

Shank: Reinforcing insert in boot sole, usually under arch of foot.

Shear strength: Measure of materials to withstand lateral shear loads; in skis, delamination is most common failure due to shear.

Shoulder: Broadest part of a ski, at the shovel.

Shovel: Upturned part of a ski tip.

SIA: Ski Industries America. Headquarters: 1200 17th Street N.W., Washington, D.C. 20036.

Side camber: Sidecut.

Sidecut: Concave curve on side profile of a ski that gives it slight hourglass shape; aids tracking and helps banked ski turn.

Sideslip: Skis gliding sideways under control.

Side walls: Sides of a ski, usually of hard material to protect more fragile core.

Silicone: Chemical polymer containing silicon and oxygen, used to waterproof leathers, fabrics, and waxless ski bases.

Sinters: Metals or plastics agglomerated by sintering: powders or pellets, sometimes of different materials, formed to solid under heat and pressure, used in metal ski pole tips and high-density plastic ski bases.

Skare: General term for hard and/or icy crust on snow.

Skating turn: Flat terrain or downhill turn; executed by one or more skating steps in new direction.

Ski striding: A variation of walking or running, done uphill on foot to imitate skiing movements.

Ski tester: Device for measuring camber stiffness, usually with electric indicators and mechanism to produce and indicate force applied.

Ski touring: Recreational cross-country skiing, usually in wilderness.

Snowmobile: Tracked motorized vehicle for travel on snow, usually with runners for steering, useful for supply transport, rescue, and pulling track setters. Recreational use curtailed or forbidden in most countries, but permitted in United States and Canada.

Snowplow: Downhill position for slowing down, stopping, and turning—ski tips together, tails apart.

Snowplow turn: Downhill turn executed in the snowplow position.

Snowshoe basket: Large accessory ski basket, fits over pole's basket for extra support on deep snow.

Soft-Lite: Trade name for synthetic boot upper textile sandwich material; has high insulation value.

Spandex: Elastic synthetic fiber, at least 85 percent polyurethane; word is anagram of *expands.*

Speed training: Physical training aimed at attaining high speed in racing.

Spinlon: Trade name for process producing elastic yarn for stretch fabrics from nylon fibers.

Spinning: (1) Process of converting short fibers into yarn. (2) Process of continuously winding fibers around ski core or ski pole mandrel prior to application of resin and subsequent hardening.

Split leather: An inside sheet of tanned cowhide split into two or more thinner layers; used in boot uppers.

Static: At a standstill. Usually an adjective, as in *weight is a static force.*

Stem turn: Downhill turn in which one ski is angled out, pointing in the new direction, to initiate the turn.

Step: (1) Stepped turn. (2) Sawtoothlike pattern embossed on waxless ski base.

Stock: British term for pole.

Strength: (1) Usually breaking strength, force required to fracture ski or pole. (2) A component of muscular fitness—the ability to lift, push, or pull against resistance.

Stride: The walklike movements that propel a skier forward.

Structural aluminum: Aluminum alloy containing magnesium, used in ski bindings.

Structural layer: Layers of a ski that carry most of the loads.

Styrene Butadiene (SB): Synthetic rubber, used in boot soles.

Super-underwear: Trade name for transport-type underwear.

Swing weight: Description of balance of ski pole.

Synthetic fabrics: Fabrics woven or knitted from yarns spun or thrown from synthetic fiber filaments.

Synthetic skis: Skis in which the structural layers are made of synthetic materials, such as fiber-plastic laminations or metal.

Tacking turn: Uphill turn connecting two traverses, done in diagonal rhythm.

Taffeta: Fine, plain-weave fabric, usually extremely lightweight, used for wind garments.

Tail: The rear end of a ski.

Tanning: Process of converting hides to leather, named for original use of vegetable tannin.

Tar: Tarlike base preparation compounds used on wood ski bases.

Telemark: (1) Region in South-central Norway. (2) Skiing position originated in Telemark: both knees bent, one leg trailing the other.

Telemark turn: A steered downhill ski turn, one of the oldest known, named for region in Norway. Characterized by little or no sideslip of skis, body in Telemark position, arms spread wide for balance.

Tempo training: Running or skiing at racing speed for periods of 10 percent to 20 percent of a race's duration.

Terry cloth: Cotton or synthetic fabric with uncut loops forming pile, used as absorbent garment lining.

Thermoplastic rubber (TR): Rubber used in injected boot soles.

Throwing: Twisting together of continuous filaments, usually of synthetic fibers, to produce yarn.

Tip: (1) Front end of a ski. (2) Bottom end of ski pole.

Tip height: Vertical height of ski tip above base with ski resting on horizontal surface.

Toe binding: Bindings that attach boots to skis by clamping front part of sole welt.

Toe insert: Reinforcing insert in toe of boot sole, usually with holes for binding pins.

Tongue: Strip of material under the lacing of a boot.

Tonkin: Bamboo cane, used for ski pole shafts, named for Gulf of Tonkin, major source.

Top grain leather: The outside, or top sheet of tanned cowhide split into two or more thinner layers, used in boot uppers and gloves.

Top sheet: (1) Upper surface sheet of synthetic ski, usually with ski cosmetics. (2) Top grain leather.

Top side length: Length from ski tip to tail, measured along top side of ski.

Torsional stiffness: Measure of a ski's resistance to twist.

Touring: (1) Cross-country skiing. (2) Heavier cross-country ski equipment, intended for wilderness use.

Touring Norm: Standard for boots and bindings, using Racing Norm profiles and Nordic Norm boot sole thicknesses, superseded in 1979 by ISO (International Standards Organization) standard.

Touring pack: Backpack used by skiers on longer tours, such as overnights.

Tow: Bundles of fiber filaments prior to spinning or throwing.

Track: (1) Path a skier has taken. (2) Prepared tracks for cross-country skiing. (3) Shouted warning, used by racer in overtaking.

Tracking: Ability of ski or pulk to follow straight course.

Track setter: Sled used to prepare ski trails and set tracks in snow, usually pulled by a snowmobile.

Training: Any physical activity that maintains or improves physical ability.

Transition snow: Snow just at freezing, in transition zone between dry and wet.

Transport-type underwear: Underwear of fabric that keeps skin dry by transporting moisture out, away from the body.

Transverse line: Line on which width of toe bindings and boot soles are measured; through outer two pins of pin binding and corresponding recesses in boot sole.

Traversing: Skiing up or down a hill on a traverse at an angle to the fall line.

Trek pack: Backpack used by skiers on extended tours.

Triathlon: Competitive skiing event comprising biathlon and Alpine giant slalom racing, usually a military ski competition event.

Tricot: Most important knit fabric for cross-country ski clothing, usually synthetic or synthetic-cotton, usually stretch.

UIPMB: Union Internationale de Pentathlon Moderne et Biathlon, the organizers of international biathlon skiing competition.

Ultron: Trade name for process producing elastic yarn for stretch fabrics from nylon fibers.

Unweighting: Taking weight off a ski.

Uphill ski: The upper ski, or the ski that finally is upper, in a ski turn.

USSA: The United States Ski Association. Headquarters: 1726 Champa Street, Suite 300, Denver, Colorado 80202.

USST: The United States Ski Team. Headquarters: Box 100, Park City, Utah 84060.

Vamp: Portion of boot upper that covers the instep of the foot.

Velcro: Trade name for nylon closure tape, in pairs, one of which consists of loops, the other of pile; tapes lock to each other with slight pressure and are opened by a firm pull.

Velour: Napped, thick cloth, usually synthetic, used in some garment linings and for ski pole grips.

Vulcanized boot: Boot with soles formed on uppers by vulcanization of rubber or synthetic rubber, usually in a sole mold.

Waxable skis: Skis whose bases are waxed for grip and glide.

Waxing iron: Iron for waxing, may be heated by flame or electricity.

Waxing torch: Small blowtorch, usually fueled by liquefied gas, used in waxing skis.

Waxless ski: Ski with irregularity in base that both grips and glides on snow without wax.

Wax remover: Solvent used to remove wax from ski bases.

Wax zone: Marked areas on ski base, for convenience in applying grip and glide waxes.

Wedge: Triangular block, usually of rubber, mounted on jumping skis under boot to increase jumper's forward lean.

Weight shift: The transfer of weight from one ski to the other. In ski strides, as in walking or running, transfer also involves dynamic (due to motion) forces in addition to body weight, so "weight shift" is strictly speaking a misleading term.

Wet-snow skis: Racing skis for use on wet snow, usually with relatively stiffer cambers, often with softer, lower-density plastic bases.

Wet-wrap: Process of wrapping fiberglass or other fibers around final core of ski or mandrel of pole, before hardening.

Wicking ability: Ability of a clothing fiber to pull and/or transport moisture.

Wide-range waxing: Wax systems for recreational skiers comprising two or three waxes, each matching a wide range of snow conditions.

Wide-track: Stance in downhill skiing, skis parallel and 4 to 12 inches apart.

Wind chill: Loss of insulating effect of air surrounding the body as wind increases.

Wood skis: Skis in which the structural layers are of wood.

World Cup: International cross-country racing competition for men and women racers. Points are awarded for a racer's best five results in nine preselected races each season: 26 points are awarded for first place, 22 for second, 19 for third, 17 for fourth, 16 for fifth, and so on, by one-point increments, down to one point for twentieth place. The skier with the most points at the end of the season is the World Cup winner. Theoretically the maximum is 130 points, corresponding to five first places.

Worsted yarn: Treated wool yarns; fibers are parallel to each other.

Woven fabric: Fabric made by weaving, process interlacing two strands of yarn, placed at right angles to each other.

Wrist strap: Strap fastened to ski pole grip, fits around wrist to prevent pole loss.

WSC: World Ski Championships, held in even-numbered years between leap years, arranged by the FIS.

XC: Common abbreviation for cross-country.

Slang is part of the living language of cross-country skiing, a varied and regional lingo, coined by skiers and ski businesspersons to speak of things for which there are yet few words in dictionaries. A sampler of cross-country ski equipment slang, from the start of the cross-country renaissance in the mid 1960s to date:

Ape: Proficient cross-country ski racer. Simile: powerful arm and leg movements apparently excel normal human ability.

Apple knickers: Baggy knickers. Descriptive: knickers appear loaded with apples, as might be stolen by small boy, character in Twain novel.

Butterscotch: Klisterwax. Simile: yellow color and taffy-like consistency.

Cosmetics: External color, pattern, or appearance of a product. Descriptive: to differentiate from internal structure or cut.

50/7, 50/12: Racing Norm 50 mm, Touring Norm 50 mm boot-binding systems. Contraction using Racing Norm boot sole thickness (7 mm) and Touring Norm boot sole thickness (12 mm).

French-Canadian Racing Gloves: Brown cotton work gloves, used by some cross-country skiers, particularly in New England. Descriptive: resemblance to gloves used by French-Canadian lumberjacks.

Glass: Fiberglass skis. Contraction.

Granola Skier: Traditionalist wilderness skier. Derogatory term, from habit of carrying granola in provisions.

Gunk: Base preparation tar. Descriptive: resemblance to compounds used to clean automobile motors.

GWM: Graduated Width Method: teaching scheme for cross-country skiing, pupil progresses from wide to narrow skis.

Hardware: Skis and ski equipment. Simile: resemblance to goods sold in hardware store, as opposed to *software* or *softgoods:* clothing.

Poon skier: Alpine skier. Derogatory term used by cross-country skiers. By rhyme with *boon* of boondocks, inferring backwardness, lack of knowledge.

Pop-up: Flexible heel plate. Descriptive: from action, flexing upwards as boot heel is lifted; motion designed to prevent icing.

Rat traps: Pin-type toe bindings with bails. Descriptive: resemblance to rat traps.

Runner: Cross-country skier, particularly a racer. Descriptive: from similar stride movements.

Skinny skis: Cross-country skis. Descriptive term used by unknowing Alpine skiers, who regard their broader, heftier skis as "regular."

Software, or soft goods: Ski clothing. Descriptive term, as opposed to *hardware,* for skis and ski equipment exclusive of clothing.

INDEX

Index of persons and organizations mentioned in the text. Excluded are companies and names of living, active ski racers and of historical persons not directly connected with skiing.

Books from The Mountaineers include:

Cross-Country Skiing

A practical guide to cross-country on the track, at the race, or in the wilds, with skills for skiing hills; teaching kids; coping with terrain, snow and weather; off-track, wilderness and expedition skiing; choosing ski equipment; waxing. By Ned Gillette, former U.S. Ski Team racer and Nordic and Alpine ski school director in Colorado, California and Vermont.
Well illustrated.

Medicine for Mountaineering

A handbook for treating accidents and illnesses in remote areas, where a physician may be several days away. Includes treatment of traumatic and environmental injuries and diseases, with particular emphasis on illnesses of high altitude or a hostile environment.

Rock Climbing

A how-to-book by Peter Livesey, one of the world's best-known rock climbers, written for the general reader. Step by step through all the latest techniques and state-of-the-art equipment. Outstanding instructional photos.

Snowshoeing

Complete information on techniques for safe, enjoyable travel in any terrain or weather; how to select, care for and use snow-shoe equipment. By Gene Prater.

The ABC of Avalanche Safety

How to spot potential avalanche areas, how to avoid one in mountain travel, how to survive if caught, how to rescue others — a handy pocket guide by Edward LaChapelle.

Mountaineering First Aid

Compact handbook for dealing with remote-area accidents and helping to prevent them. Excellent text for outdoor safety or first-aid classes. Covers immediate care for common emergencies, plus preparation for rescue or evacuation. By Dick Mitchell.

Mountains of the World

All the major mountains and hundreds of out-of-the-way peaks and ranges, from the Alps to Antarctica, from Everest to Ecuador, from the Cascades to the Caucasus. Route descriptions, history, local color by William Bueler.

The Mountains of Canada

Over 100 magnificent color photos by some of the most talented photographers in North America. Author Randy Morse, himself a climber, sees mountains in terms of their relationship to modern man. He includes, to counterpoint the photos, fascinating stories of climbers as they faced the challenge of these peaks.

K2 — The Savage Mountain

The second highest mountain in the world long withheld its summit from American climbers. Probably the best remembered expedition to K2 was in 1953, led by Charles Houston and Robert Bates. They told the engrossing story in this classic of mountaineering literature. This reprint also includes retrospective essays by expedition members.

Gervasutti's Climbs

The autobiography of one of the leading Italian mountaineers of the 1930s, who made many first ascents in the Western Alps. Gervasutti writes with a depth of detail, yet with a degree of introspection that will interest mountaineers of all generations.

The Last Blue Mountain

The mountain was Haramosh, a lesser known but thoroughly challenging peak in the Himalaya. The expedition was an adventurous reconnaissance until, suddenly, a fall through a cornice led to a series of incredible disasters. This book leads to a nerve-wrenching conclusion you'll never forget. By Ralph Barker.

Tales of A Western Mountaineer

Complete reprint of a rare (1924) account by C.E. Rusk, who made a number of first-ascents on Northwest mountains and named major glaciers on Mt. Adams and Glacier Peak.

The Unknown Mountain

A mountain literature classic, long out of print: Don Munday's story of the discovery and exploration of ice-tipped Mt. Waddington and other peaks of the B.C. Coast Range. These trips were made in the 1920s and 1930s, through rugged unmapped terrain, without benefit of today's lightweight gear.

100 Hikes in the Alps

A well-illustrated guide to the best hikes in a number of Alpine valleys, in Yugoslavia, Austria, Italy, France, Switzerland and Germany, plus selected areas of the Pyrenees. Maps, photos.

. . .plus regional hiking and climbing guides on Washington, British Columbia and Alaska

For a complete list of books, write The Mountaineers, 719 Pike Street, Seattle, Washington 98101.